THE
LANGUAGE
— OF —
LEADERSHIP

IT'S MORE THAN JUST TALK

PAUL E. TSIKA

DESTINY IMAGE® PUBLISHERS, INC.
P.O. Box 310, Shippensburg, PA 17257-0310
"Promoting Inspired Lives."

This book and all other Destiny Image and Destiny Image Fiction books are available at Christian bookstores and distributors worldwide.

Cover design by Eileen Rockwell
Interior design by Terry Clifton

For more information on foreign distributors, call 717-532-3040.
Reach us on the Internet: www.destinyimage.com.

ISBN 13 TP: 978-0-7684-5552-6
ISBN 13 eBook: 978-0-7684-5553-3
ISBN 13 HC: 978-0-7684-5555-7
ISBN 13 LP: 978-0-7684-5554-0

For Worldwide Distribution, Printed in the U.S.A.
1 2 3 4 5 6 7 8 / 25 24 23 22 21 20

Dedication

Some of the greatest leaders I've ever known personally are the leaders of World Wide Dream Builders.

The Diamonds of World Wide know that talk is cheap but decisive action is really the "Language of Leadership."

I have watched many of them grow, mature and change to become the great leaders they are today.

They are loved, honored, valued and respected by tens of thousands of people around the world.

They have raised the bar of faith, work ethic and consistency with a "never give up" attitude that has inspired millions.

One of my mentors taught me, "There's no such thing as a great man of God. There's only a great God in yielded men."

I believe that. In like manner great leadership is not a given because of position. It's earned day by day in the trenches of life.

These men and women have earned their position by serving others, yielding to what's right and never settling for less than God's best.

So it is with great enthusiasm that I dedicate "The Language of Leadership" to my friends, the great Diamond leaders of World Wide Dream Builders.

They don't only speak the language, they do the work to earn the title of leadership.

ACKNOWLEDGMENTS

My staff: Thom and Kelly, Mark and Gretchen and Jennifer who keep me on course and on task every day. Without their faithful, encouraging support, I would not be able to stay in my lane. Thank you for having a "We got this" attitude and work ethic.

Destiny Image: John Martin and Meelika Marzzarella along with your amazing, efficient staff. You all make writing and publishing books a delightful experience from beginning to end. Thank you.

Dr. J. Tod Zeiger: A fellow laborer in God's work who is always there for me. His insights, gifts, and passions have been of immeasurable help to me with my writings. Tod is one of the most gifted communicators of God's Word I've ever been on a platform with. He's a brother in Christ, a fellow pastor, part of my staff, and my dear friend for years (jtzeiger@aol.com).

Billie Kaye: I have been greatly blessed with a really good and godly wife. I would only recommend that you read her new book, *Priceless,* to understand why I will always acknowledge her in everything I do. Thank you BK, for always being faithful to every part of who we are as a couple. I love you. You truly do complete me.

CONTENTS

PREFACE

Recently I heard a quote from Supreme Court Justice John Roberts about leadership. He said, "When you're holding the reins of leadership you should be careful not to tug on them too much. You may find out they're not connected to anything." What wise insight about leadership.

Perhaps this is why some leaders move from a servant leadership position to a controlling leadership position. Whenever they've tugged too often and found there's nothing connected at the other end, they panic. That panic is more often than not about losing that leadership influence. And influence is everything in leadership. But there's a world of difference between influence through serving and influence through intimidation.

That difference is at the very heart of this book, *The Language of Leadership*.

The definition of the word *language* from the *Merriam-Webster Dictionary* is "the words, their pronunciation, and the methods of combining them used and understood by a community." The community, in this case, that I want to communicate with is the leadership community. Leadership does have, in my opinion, a unique and specific culture, people, and language. Throughout this book you will find thought-provoking attitude adjustments, insightful simple steps to take, and common community language all leaders employ.

I will not leave you guessing about successful leadership and your responsibility to grow into that role. Hopefully this will not be just another book you purchase and put away—it will be a life-impacting read and application for you, your team, and your future.

PAUL TSIKA
Restoration Ranch

Great Leaders Know How to Stay Positive in a Negative World

Finally, brothers and sisters, whatever is true, whatever is noble, whatever is right, whatever is pure, whatever is lovely, whatever is admirable—if anything is excellent or praiseworthy—think about such things.

—Philippians 4:8

Having a more productive attitude doesn't mean you won't still encounter obstacles. However, the way you approach these obstacles will be more pro-active and self-directed. The better your attitude, the better you will communicate.

—Deborah Day[1]

Introduction

King Solomon said:

> *Keep vigilant watch over your heart; that's where life starts. Don't talk out of both sides of your mouth; avoid*

3

careless banter, white lies, and gossip. Keep your eyes straight ahead; ignore all sideshow distractions. Watch your step, and the road will stretch out smooth before you. Look neither right nor left; leave evil in the dust (Proverbs 4:23-27 MSG).

I would say that is pretty good advice, but one of the most challenging things to do.

Leaders are particularly susceptible to a negative attitude because everyone expects nothing but positive and constructive words to come out of their mouths. I have found one of the most difficult things to do is to keep your head on straight while the circumstances around you are filled with negativity.

There are times when it is just easier to go with the flow rather than rock the boat. Vocabulary.com defines negativity as: a tendency to be downbeat, disagreeable, and skeptical. It's a pessimistic attitude that always expects the worst.[2]

Trying to keep a positive outlook in a *negative* atmosphere does not happen by wishful thinking or burying your head in the sand and hoping things get better. Changing negative circumstances into a positive environment takes a proactive approach that can lead to a positive outcome. Changes in any organizational structure—that make a lasting impact—must come from the top.

Author Terry Orlick, PhD, observed: "My greatest power in life is my power to choose. I am the final authority over me. I make me."[3] According to that statement, I can choose to do something to change, or not; it is all up to me. The process of change starts with one person—*you!*

Ask yourself the following four questions:

1. What am I doing right now to communicate to those around me the importance of creating a positive climate?

2. Have I allowed negativity to stifle the growth of our organization? If so, what am I going to do about it?

3. Am I afraid to confront those who have fostered a negative atmosphere for fear of losing them?

4. Once the decision is made to take action, am I willing to fight through the obstacles to reach my destination?

I don't believe we are born with a negative disposition. It is a learned behavior. From the earliest stages of our development, our brains are being programmed. Most people have no clue what the brain is capable of achieving. If what the experts tell us is true, that we are only using a small percentage of our brain's capability, then we are missing out on the greatest super-computer ever created!

Did you know?

- The brain is about 2 percent of your body weight.
- The brain consumes about 20-30 percent of the body's energy.
- There are about 100 billion neurons in the brain.
- Each neuron or nerve cell is connected to other nerve cells in the brain.
- There are over 1,000,000,000,000,000 connections in the brain.
- Each neuron is capable of storing knowledge.
- The brain acts as "master control" over our actions, emotions, and feelings.

Three Sources of Negativity

1. The Environment Around Us

I am sure you would agree that it is easier to find more negative news than positive. We are living in a 24/7 stream of news, breaking stories, and cryptic comments on all platforms of social media. If we are not careful, we will allow into our minds far more of the negative than we realize.

> A man's mind may be likened to a garden, which may be intelligently cultivated or allowed to run wild; but whether cultivated or neglected, it must, and will, bring forth. If no useful seeds are put into it, then an abundance of useless weed seeds will fall therein, and will continue to produce their kind.
>
> —JAMES ALLEN[4]

2. Painful Experiences Behind Us

Many people are controlled by their past. If that past was filled with negative experiences, then it's easy to understand why they have such a sour outlook on life. Refusing to "let go" and allow healing to take place, the wounds of past hurt will continue to fester into a poison that will affect the entire body, soul, and spirit.

In my book *Sequoia-Size Success*, I wrote the following about "Healing Deep Wounds":

> Getting burned in relationships and bruised in our hearts is an inescapable reality of life. However, if wrongly treated, these wounds will lead us into bondage to bitterness. When we get burned in a relationship, we do our best to keep from falling apart, losing our minds or reacting in

a way that would increase the pain by public embarrassment. We commonly do this by wrapping the wound or bruise in a psychological bandage of suppression that does one of three things:

1. We either assume all the blame and shame and say to ourselves, "You're a bad person and deserve this."

2. We internalize the hurt and trauma to such an extent that it causes an emotional overload and little, or no feelings are experienced.

3   We assert control and develop either an "I'm standing on the inside, and nothing you can do on the outside will make me sit down" attitude.

Wrapping a wound in any of the above bandages provides only temporary relief. Why? They only hide the hurt and shut out any of the healing light of God's Word.[5]

3. *A System of Error Within Us*

If you are what you eat, then it is logical to believe you act out what you think. The author of Proverbs tells us, *"as he thinks in his heart, so is he"* (Proverbs 23:7 NKJV).

It is a proven fact that you will eventually become and behave the way you think. A successful leader cannot be double-minded. As the old saying goes, "Garbage in, and garbage out!" When you spend your time surrounded by negative, fearful thoughts, you cannot expect success.

Consider: If you are always waiting for the "other shoe to drop," it probably will. If you have already decided that every event in your life is filled with the possibility of defeat instead of victory, you will be trapped in the black hole of negativity—from which it is hard to escape!

I have met many people who view life the same way as the fictional character George in the comedy series, *Seinfeld:*

> George speaking with his therapist*:* "God would never let me be successful. He'd kill me first. He'll never let me be happy."
>
> Therapist: "I thought you didn't believe in God?"
>
> George: "I do for the bad things."[6]

In a recent edition of *Mindvalley Blog,* author Christie Marie Sheldon gave her readers a negativity test. I took it; now it's your turn.

> Quiz to gauge the level of negative energy within you:
>
> - Do you complain? All the time or just sometimes?
> - Do you often discuss what's wrong in the world more than what's right? This includes the "terrible" weather, "horrible" traffic, "idiotic" government, "lousy" economy, "stupid" in-laws, etc.
> - Do you criticize? All the time or just certain people?
> - Are you attracted to drama and disaster (can you unglue yourself from the TV when there's a news story of a disaster and can you avoid getting involved in the lives of dysfunctional celebrities)?
> - Do you blame? All the time or just certain situations?
> - Do you believe that you have no control over most of your results?
> - Do you feel like a victim? Do you talk about people doing things to you?

- Are you grateful for what is, or will you be grateful when things finally start going right for you?
- Do you feel like things are happening to you? Or do you feel that they are happening through you?

The last two points are important: If you're not grateful except when things go right, you are negative.[7]

Keep your thoughts positive because your thoughts become your words. Keep your words positive because your words become your behavior. Keep your behavior positive because your behavior becomes your habits. Keep your habits positive because your habits become your values. Keep your values positive because your values become your destiny.

—MAHATMA GANDHI[8]

Five Strategies That Change a Negative into a Positive

1. Face forward

Every car is equipped with a rearview mirror. The purpose is simple—to see what is approaching you from behind and warn you of impending trouble. But, you don't drive forward always looking behind you in your rearview mirror. If you did, you would eventually crash.

Some people live their lives always looking in the rearview mirror of past defeats, failures, and mistakes. I like the attitude of apostle Paul who decided that his full potential could never be reached as long as he dwelt on the past and never moved forward into his destiny. He says in Philippians 3:12-13 (NLV):

I do not say that I have received this or have already become perfect. But I keep going on to make that life my own as Christ Jesus made me His own. No, Christian brothers, I do not have that life yet. But I do one thing. I forget everything that is behind me and look forward to that which is ahead of me.

2. *Determine what you want*

I have never met a person with a negative outlook who actually knew what he or she wanted out of life. If people do not know what they want and what they are willing to do to go full speed ahead, how can they face life with a positive attitude? And, how can you lead someone else to a life of success if you don't know where you are going yourself?

Author Richie Norton gave interesting snapshots of three types of people who want success.

> People who want success fall into three categories:
>
> *Wishers* want things to be different and wait patiently for that successful change to come. They believe in magic fairies.
>
> *Worriers* fear the worst and imagine all the terrible things that are going to happen if things don't change. They believe in monsters.
>
> *Warriors* take action on their wishes, slay the dragons of their worries, and fight for their lives. They believe in work.
>
> Which one are you?
>
> If you want to transform your life or business, be a warrior.[9]

Based on Norton's assessment, which one are you? Don't allow others to decide your future. Never settle for less, period. The best is waiting for those who will plan and take action on their future.

3. *Choose your attitude*

There are some things in life you can't change. For instance, you didn't choose your parents, where you were born, or your skin color. What's the use in complaining about things that you had no control over. But there is one thing you can choose—*your attitude!*

Stop a minute and consider just a few things you can choose:

- You can choose what books you will read over the next twelve months.

- You can choose what types of entertainment you will allow into your mind.

- You can choose who you will allow access to your life.

- You can choose to approach each new day with a positive or negative attitude.

- You can choose not to allow circumstances to determine your attitude.

Most if not all leadership teachers will tell you there is a fine line between winning and losing in life. Sitting on that razor-thin line is one word—*attitude*. Winston Churchill said, "Attitude is a little thing that makes a big difference."

The following are a few of the differences between a negative and a positive attitude:

- A negative attitude finds a way to blame others for all mistakes.

- A positive attitude steps up and takes responsibility for mistakes.

- A negative attitude becomes an expert at making excuses.

- A positive attitude moves beyond excuses and gets the job done.

- A negative attitude allows obstacles to stop progress toward the goal.

- A positive attitude views every obstacle as an opportunity to learn, grow, and move forward in spite of the challenge.

If you were hiring someone, which type of person would you choose?

Applicant 1: This person has excellent skills, plenty of job experience, and a quality four-year education. But in the interview process, you notice this person does not demonstrate a positive outlook on life in general.

Applicant 2: This person has limited skills, minimal job experience, and a two-year college degree. But in the interview process, you can tell this person has a can-do attitude with a willingness to get the job done. All this candidate wants is a chance.

I don't know about you, but I'm choosing applicant 2. Why? You can take someone with a positive attitude and add the necessary skill and knowledge needed to do the job. But trying to rearrange a negative attitude while keeping the organization from being infected is a tall order. I will take the positive over the negative every time, wouldn't you?

4. *Learn to laugh*

I have never read an article that stated a negative approach to life is right for your overall well-being. On the other hand, there are dozens, probably hundreds, of articles, books, and tapes that teach us that a well-rounded life includes humor and laughter. There is nothing new about that fact; as a matter of fact, there is an ancient proverb that says, *"A glad heart makes a happy face, but when the heart is sad, the spirit is broken"* (Proverbs 15:13 NLV). Even the ancients knew the benefits of a good laugh!

I read an article titled, "Laughter is the Best Medicine: The Health Benefits of Humor and Laughter." The article asked and answered the question, "Why is laughter the sweetest medicine for mind and body?" The answer:

> Laughter is a powerful antidote to stress, pain, and conflict. Nothing works faster or more dependably to bring your mind and body back into balance than a good laugh. Humor lightens your burdens, inspires hopes, connects you to others, and keeps you grounded, focused, and alert. It also helps you to release anger and be more forgiving.
>
> With so much power to heal and renew, the ability to laugh easily and frequently is a tremendous resource for surmounting problems, enhancing your relationships, and supporting both physical and emotional health. Best of all, this priceless medicine is fun, free, and easy to use.[10]

5. *Look around you.*

I can tell a great deal about a person just by knowing who their friends are, and who has access to their life. I don't know many people who hang around with others who do not share a common interest. Your circle of friends like what you like and do things you want to do. Your destiny is significantly determined by the circle of friends allowed in your sphere of influence.

When you allow someone access to your life, you are allowing that person the right to interact with and influence you in ways that no one else can. The point is, you don't have to let negative people and unhealthy influences into your life.

- *Some people are like parasites, so remove them quickly.* When a parasite is discovered in the body, the only remedy is to remove it at any cost. Although the danger may go undetected for some time, eventually it will cause damage to internal organs, even to the point of death. As painful as it may be to remove certain friends from having access to you, keep in mind their negativity will pose a serious risk to your mental, emotional, and spiritual health. Parasites have one unique quality that stands alone—they can suck the life right out of you before you even realize what they have done!

- *Some people are like piranhas, so don't go in the water.* A piranha is known to be one of the world's most ferocious fish, with razor-sharp teeth, and a biting ability to rip apart and devour even the biggest prey that might wander into its killing zone. The number one advice given to those who think it might be fun to travel to South America and swim with the piranhas is, DON'T! The same advice is given to those who think that allowing someone who is continuously "ripping apart" others to be nothing more than a harmless activity. You must protect your dreams and visions by refusing to allow a piranha relationship to continue. It is not harmless or benign.

▪ *Some people are pretenders, so don't play their game.* Some people are like waterboys on the football team. As soon as you get "hot" about your future, they love to throw cold water in your face! They pretend to be your friend as long as you stay on the same level. But as soon as you determine to move ahead, they are standing by to pour negative words to bring you back down to earth. The mask of pretention is lifted as soon as they unload on you.

Make up your mind to want only those people around you who God has ordained to come into your sphere of influence. Don't allow the negative dream thieves to crowd out those who can help you reach your life goals.

> People who think they can control their negative emotions and manifest them when they want to, simply deceive themselves. Negative emotions depend on identification; if identification is destroyed in some particular case, they disappear. The strangest and most fantastic fact about negative emotions is that people actually worship them.
>
> —P.D. Ouspensky[11]

As the old saying goes, "There are two ways to learn, by mistakes or mentors." I have learned many life lessons from both, but my choice will always be a coach or a mentor who can point me in the right direction. You must find people who will not only celebrate who you are but will have the courage to challenge you in your progress.

A trusted friend is like a cheerleader on the sidelines, cheering your accomplishments. But the last time I looked, cheerleaders don't send in plays to win the game. You need a wise and experienced coach for that. We need both to succeed in life.

A Final Thought

These five strategies—along with a grateful attitude, a self-disciplined lifestyle, and viewing opportunities through the looking-glass of problems—will eventually turn any negative situation into a positive.

In case you think that your situation can never be turned around, consider the story of what many consider the greatest basketball player of all time:

> Michael Jordon redefined the NBA, and by acclamation is the greatest basketball player of all time. In his sophomore year he was not accepted on his varsity basketball team, because he was too short and clumsy to play the game.
>
> That was the day he went home locked himself in his room, and cried for hours. But instead of quitting he focused on the game, and developed basketball skills at an unbelievable level.
>
> He later went on to play for the Chicago Bulls with 6 championships, 5 league MVP's, 10 scoring titles, and 14 All-Star Selections which places his legacy as the best player ever.

Michael Jordon failed before success over, and over along the way, but still managed to have the greatest career in basketball history.

"I've missed more than 9,000 shots in my career. I've lost almost 300 games. Twenty-six times, I've been trusted to take the game winning shot and missed. I've failed over and over and over again in my life. And that is why I succeed."

—MICHAEL JORDON.[12]

Remember, your leadership journey is never over until *you say it is!*

2

GREAT LEADERS REFLECT A FATHER'S/MOTHER'S HEART

As a father has compassion on his children, so the Lord has compassion on those who fear him.

—PSALM 103:13

You don't raise heroes, you raise sons. And if you treat them like sons, they'll turn out to be heroes, even if it's just in your own eyes.

—WALTER M. SCHIRRA SR.[1]

Introduction

I don't know of any father who starts with the idea of winning the "lousiest father of the year award." Most, if not all, picture themselves as a "super-dad" with the power of raising their sons and daughters to become well-adjusted, productive members of society. But, as we all know, life can sneak up on us without warning and throw our dream of becoming a perfect father into a downward spiral. Before we know it, a super-dad turns into a super-dud. Why? Let me suggest three underlying causes:

1. *Unrealistic expectations:* A desire to be the perfect father is a great goal, but unrealistic. There are no perfect dads, period. All of us who are fathers have our flaws, faults, and failures. Realizing our humanity is the first step to an honest approach to fatherhood.

2. *Unrealized dreams:* Most fathers have dreams. Having a vision for their family, finances, and the future are all worthy of expending brain power. Tragically, I have watched up close, and personal fathers push their sons into something simply to live their dreams through them. Many times, this "push" plays out in sports.

Kent Sanders wrote an article explaining why he won't force his son to play sports. In the article, he states: "I don't have anything against sports. However, I do have a serious problem with a culture that defines a boy's masculinity by his involvement and success in sports."

Sanders continues: "I want him to know that I don't measure my worth by his accomplishments. Every good father wants his son to succeed in life. But we must always check our motives. Do we want our sons to succeed for their sake, or for our sake? We've all seen fathers who are living vicariously through their sons, trying to recapture the glory days of their youth through their sons' achievements. We must make sure we are not compensating for our own insecurities by pushing our sons to climb higher and go further than we did."[2]

3. *Unmet goals:* Planning for the future and setting goals are good things, but more than one dad has given up on life because they didn't become millionaires by the time they reached the age of thirty! Somehow in the

rush and pressure of life, they forgot the most significant return on investment is the deposit placed in their children's lives, not in their portfolio.

The Core Issues We Face

There is a breakdown between the "ideal" and the "reality" when it comes to fathers and sons. There may be many underlying issues, but I see two core issues at the top of the list. I call these twin evils, *The Entertainment Effect* and *The Cultural Effect.*

The Entertainment Effect

The issue of, "How much does the entertainment world" affect our society has been raging for decades. On one side are those who believe that the world of Hollywood only reflects what is going on in society. On the other hand, are those who believe that society is influenced by what entertainment gives them through movies, television, and the video industry. The debate will never be won—both sides are sticking to their opinions.

But unless you have been living on another planet without access to a television, you know that fathers in the United States have been "dumbed down" to the point of embarrassment. We no longer sit and watch Ward Cleaver, the father on *Leave it to Beaver,* smoke his pipe and look bemused at the fumbling and bumbling of his sons, Wally and the Beave. Today we are offered a steady portrayal of dads who are incompetent, stupid, lazy, fat, and incapable of taking care of the family.

A quick sample:

* Popular television shows in the 1950s and '60s included *Leave it to Beaver, The Donna Reed Show,*

The Rifleman, The Andy Griffith Show, and *Father Knows Best.* All of these shows portrayed the father as a strong but compassionate figure who led his family with core values of morality and decency. They were not perfect, all had flaws; but they were always out front leading the family for everyone's best interest at heart.

- In the 1970s and '80s, TV sit-coms included *The Cosby Show, Growing Pains, Family Ties.* Again, for the most part, the dads were portrayed as leaders in the home.

- But as we moved into the 1990s and onward, the trend of dads being disrespected and treated as dimwits started and has been going downhill ever since: *Married with Children; The Simpsons; King of Queens; Everybody Loves Raymond.* And, so many more. It is now hard to find anything produced by the media that gives an accurate picture of what a real dad looks like.

John Tierney wrote an opinion piece published in *The New York Times* titled "The Doofus Dad." A portion follows:

"Where did we fathers go wrong? We spend twice as much time with our kids as we did two decades ago, but on television we're oblivious ('Jimmy Neutron'), troubled ('The Sopranos'), deranged ('Malcolm in the Middle') and generally incompetent ('Everybody Loves Raymond'). Even if Dad has a good job, like the star of 'Home Improvement,' at home he's forever making messes that must be straightened out by Mom."[3]

Not only are dads portrayed as idiots in sitcoms, but TV commercials add fuel the bonfire of disrespect. Seth Stevenson writes, "Ad after ad makes doltish Dad the butt of all jokes. He's outwitted by his children. He's the target of condescending eye rolls from his wife. He's a dumb, incompetent, sometimes even selfish oaf—but his family loves him anyway."[4]

For example, a Huggies diapers commercial which aired in 2012 stated, "To prove Huggies can handle just about anything, we put them to the toughest test imaginable: dads, alone with their babies, in one house, for five days." The assumption that dads can't take care of their own children was offensive to one man in particular. Chris Routly was a stay-at-home dad who decided to take action. After viewing the Huggies commercial, Routly put together a petition on Change.org. In his statement, Routly wrote, "Why not find a way to celebrate dads in a way that doesn't minimize, stereotype and judge us as—at best—well-meaning but second-class parents?" Epilogue: "Within a week of Routly posting his petition...Kimberly-Clark executives got on the phone with him and promised to modify their campaign. They pulled the ad with the dads watching sports and replaced it with a spot showing tender moments between fathers and infants."[5]

Sadly, we are living in a generation that does not believe that fathers are necessary to the well-being of their children—*especially the father-son relationship.* It is not at all uncommon for children to be raised in homes where no father is present.

From the very beginning of creation, we were given the "role" of the man as he relates to the woman and his children. The Scripture tells us, *"For this reason a man will leave his father and his mother, and will be joined to his wife. And they will become one flesh"* (Genesis 2:24 NLV).

One of the most important aspects of a dad's contribution to the lives of his kids lies precisely in what Dr. David Popenoe, Professor of Sociology at Rutgers University and Co-Director of the National Marriage Project, calls his "significantly different parenting style." Men and women are different, and as a result mothers and fathers parent their children differently. It should be obvious that, as a man, you are in a position to exert a specifically masculine influence upon your son.

Dr. Popenoe has this to say about the importance of a father's role in the family:

> Fathers are far more than just "second adults" in the home. Involved fathers-especially biological fathers-bring positive benefits to their children that no other person is as likely to bring. They provide protection and economic support and male role models. They have a parenting style that is significantly different from that of a mother and that difference is important in healthy child development.[6]

The Cultural Effect

Although it garners very little press, the statistics bear out the fact that fatherless homes are a national tragedy and fast becoming a national emergency. The following are ten facts I gleaned from an informative article titled *The Importance of Fathers (According to Science).*

1. Children with fathers are less likely to live in poverty.

2. Children with fathers do better in school.

3. Children without fathers are more likely to do jail time.

4. Children with fathers are less likely to abuse drugs and alcohol.

5. Children without fathers are more likely to be sexually active as teenagers.

6. Children without fathers are more likely to be obese.

7. Children with fathers are more likely to have a larger vocabulary.

8. Children with fathers get more roughhousing (and roughhousing makes kids awesome).

9. Children with fathers are more likely to be encouraged to take healthy risks.

10. Children with fathers gain many additional benefits to health and happiness.[7]

Did you know that the majority of mass shootings that have taken place are committed by young men who come from fatherless homes? No matter how much the media ignores the problem, the facts are clear.

Matt Walsh wrote in an article for the *Daily Wire* stating:

Over 60% of youth suicides are from fatherless homes. Over 80% of youths in prison are from fatherless homes. Over 70% of high school dropouts are from fatherless homes. Over 70% of kids in drug abuse treatment centers are from fatherless homes. The fatherless home epidemic is a verified national emergency, and should be treated as such. But the fatherless factor is just one part of the equation. The other part is that nearly all of the kids who fall into these statistics are boys. Pretty much every mass shooter in American history, with very rare exception, has been male. 93% of the inmates in federal prison are men. 90% of murders are committed by men. The vast majority of rapists and child molesters are male. Men are three times more likely to kill themselves.[8]

Our culture has changed so much in the past fifty years that it is no wonder young men have grown up to believe that "nothing lasts forever," including a stable home life. It is a genetic fact that boys are wired to emulate their dads. If the model set before them was one of an "absentee" father, whether physically or emotionally, somehow the son thinks this is the rule, not the exception.

Many experts have concluded that the significant problems of our day can be traced to fathers who have abandoned their responsibilities. As the old saying goes, "Any male can produce a son, but it takes a real man to become a father!"

According to Rick Johnson, author of *Better Dads, Stronger Sons* and founder of Better Dads:

> One of the reasons I think has to do with our culture's mentality in general. Our culture now has more of an instant gratification kind of mentality. When I talk to young people, they're frankly a little bit hopeless that marriage can last for a long time. It's because they've experienced growing up in a culture of divorce. Why we're seeing more of it now is because clearly, the role models we have growing up are things that we tend to emulate. When people have been brought up in a broken home, or a fatherless environment, boys tend to model that

behavior, sometimes unconsciously. A lot of men vow to never leave their wife or children, yet because they've kind of been programmed that way, they're almost helpless to be able to stop a chain of events that leads to that kind of conclusion.[9]

Our so-called modern culture, that has an answer for everything, has determined the best way to fix the "fatherless effect" is one of two ways:

1. Use any means necessary to downplay the importance of having a father in the home. Begin at kindergarten age and teach children that there are no such things as roles in the home. Men are nothing more than sperm donors. And as soon as we can figure out how to manufacture sperm in a test tube, we won't need men at all, except to work themselves into a stress-related heart attack, or die in a war.

2. The "wussification" of our sons is on the agenda of the progressive movement. According to the Urban Dictionary, a "wuss" is "a person who is physically weak and ineffectual. Often a male person with low courage factor."[10]

Will Leitch, wrote an article that was published in *New York Magazine,* titled, "How to Raise a Boy," and his premise is very clear: "It is time to change the landscape of America with respect to how we raise our sons."[11] He is advocating a weaker role for men, who, according to his article are responsible for the majority of problems we are facing today. Sorry Mr. Leitch, but this author strongly *disagrees!*

Cure for a Fatherless Generation

Regardless of a changing society mixed with the pressure to conform to a new standard of conduct based on liberal, progressive thinking that is blurring the lines of male and female roles, it is time to recapture the hearts of our sons.

Maybe you didn't have a father who took time with you or gave you the positive reinforcement that you needed. Not having a dad who presented a positive role model is no longer an excuse for you to neglect your son. The cycle of negativity can be broken by one generation who will stand up and declare that, "Just because 'bad' things happened to me in my childhood, is not a reason to pass it on to my sons!"

Two critical things you can do:

1. Be a positive role model.

"Don't do as I do, but do as I say" doesn't work anymore. Kids are not oblivious to what goes on inside the home. The facts bear out the truth that sons will emulate the behavior of their fathers. If sons see their father treat their mother like a slave, bully and abuse her, physically and emotionally harm her and the kids, then the chances are those sons will grow up and treat their wife and kids the same way. I once saw a meaningful plaque stating: "The greatest gift a father can give to his children is to demonstrate love to their mother." The keyword is "demonstrate."

2. Take the time to mentor your son.

Everyone needs a mentor or a coach to help them become all they were created to be. A wise father will take the time to impart wisdom nuggets that will enrich his son for a lifetime.

My father didn't tell me how to live; he lived, and let me watch him do it.

—Clarence Budington Kelland[12]

10 Things I Wish Every Father Would Say to His Son

1. *Growing your muscles is okay.* I know it is part of your DNA to want to grow strong and fit. I'm okay with that, but don't forget the *one* muscle that you will need to exercise to find success in life—your BRAIN! Determine to be a lifelong learner. Yes, there are things you can learn every day of your life if you will open your eyes and ears. God gave you two ears, two eyes, and only one mouth for a reason. Learn to be a wise man, not a wise guy!

2. *Nobody likes a bully.* I would never encourage you to start a fight, but if you see someone being bullied, you have my permission to step in and stop it. Aggressive behavior is part of a young man's makeup, but it is never an excuse for taking advantage of someone who is more passive than you. Learn to channel your aggression into something positive, not negative.

3. *You don't have to have all the answers.* I know when you were young, you thought *I* had all the answers. As you get older, you might think *you* have all the answers. The truth is, no one has *all* the answers to all of life's questions. The bottom line is, don't depend on others to always tell you what to do. If you want to know something, ask someone who has traveled the road longer than you. That's an excellent place to start.

4. *Treat women the same way you would want your mother treated.* Son, women are a mystery that will never be solved, but that doesn't lessen the idea that they must be treated with honor and respect. One day the Lord will see fit to give you a wife, and you must remember that she is not your maid or your slave, but a partner for life. Marriage is a two-way street. Never verbally, physically, or emotionally mistreat a woman. If you want respect from her, give it first, and watch what will happen.

5. *Nobody likes a dead fish, so don't shake hands like one!* When you meet people, look them in the eye and give a firm handshake. Having good manners and making a good appearance does not make you less of a man. Remember son, people will treat you the way you present yourself to them. If you look like a reprobate, chances are they will treat you like one. There are times and places for everything; learn the difference.

6. *Watch for stumps when you jump out of the boat.* Another part of your DNA is the need for an adventure to live. I get that. There are going to be plenty of times when you will want to take a risk and jump out of the boat. All I ask is to make sure you know where the stumps are before you do.

7. *Lose the losers and find the winners.* You can always tell who and what you are by the friends you keep. If your circle of friends is going in a different direction from where you want to go, then lose them. Your future is too important to run after people who don't share your

dreams. If they choose to walk away, let them walk. If you have to beg people to be your friend, they don't belong to you to begin with, so let them go. And don't discount your spiritual side. Yes, making moral and ethical judgments springs from a spiritual compass inside you. My counsel is to find the Lord, give Him a place in your life, and never let go.

8. *The light is always on.* My love for you is nonnegotiable, and there is nothing you can do or say that will change that. I'm sure I disappointed my dad, and there will be times you might disappoint me, but know this—the light will always be on, and I will never turn my back on you. Our relationship is never open for debate. I'm not perfect, but I'll always be your dad.

9. *Invest in someone's success.* There is an old saying that tells us whatever you make happen for someone else, the Lord will make happen for you. I somehow believe that statement is true. You are never wrong to invest your time, energy, and even money to help someone establish themselves. Focusing attention on others is a source of joy and does not take away from your success. Another person's blessings are never your loss.

10. *You are a priority to me.* There have been times when I have allowed the pressure (of ministry or my career) to draw me away from you. It may have appeared that I gave you the scraps of my time, but please never think you don't matter to me—because you do! Everything about you is valuable. Whether it is a school project, sports, or your friends, I want you to know that what

is important to you, it is important to me. My greatest joy is to include you in everything I do—because I am proud to call you my son, and I am proud when you call me your dad!

A Final Thought

We have the greatest book ever penned on how to form a positive relationship with our sons—the Bible. Within its pages are golden nuggets that help us avoid the things that are tearing families apart—especially the father-son relationship. If we avail ourselves to God's wisdom, our society would be healed.

This chapter focused on fathers and sons, so I can't leave this discussion without sharing with you the greatest demonstration of a father's heart ever written. The familiar story is found in Luke 15:11-32. I urge you to stop and read the passage now.

Some have said this account of a wayward son is the greatest short story ever written showing God's love for us. Jesus gave many details lending to the idea that He was telling an event that actually happened. Either way, it's a remarkable story that demonstrated the love of a father for his sons.

From my viewpoint, much of the retelling of the story has a misplaced focus. The story is really about a father's love for his son, not the fact that his rebellious son went into the "far" country, wasted his inheritance, and then came home. Many a wayward son has come home only to find the lights have been turned off and a once loving father's heart had grown cold. Not so here!

Six Important Life Nuggets
From Luke 15:11-32

1. *A father has an open-door policy.* An open-door policy doesn't mean the father approved of his son's attitude or behavior. But he knew that one day his son would realize his mistake and return to his rightful place. In reality, what we are saying is our wayward children can always "come home" to the father's house. The lights will always be on. If we turn off the lights, literally or figuratively, we may miss a golden opportunity to see our children restored.

2. *A father prays for his children.* I can imagine that every day the father would make his way out to the gate looking down the dusty road for any sign of his son. No doubt as each day turned into a week and then a month, or even a year, the father patiently, lovingly, expectantly, and hopefully waited and prayed for his son to come home.

    One night a father overheard his son pray: Dear God, make me the kind of man my Daddy is. Later that night, the Father prayed: Dear God, make me the kind of man my son believes I am.

    —AUTHOR UNKNOWN

3. *A father has compassion for his children.* "*So he got up and went to his father. But while he was still a long way off, his father saw him and was filled with compassion for him*" (Luke 15:20). *Compassion* literally means "to suffer together." The father was hurting alongside his son. No, he wasn't in the pigpen with him, but he felt the

anguish and despair as though he were there. Instead of punishing his son, the father's compassion led him to relieve his son's suffering. The son left the father's house saying give me...give me...and now he's saying help me...help me! What a difference in attitude.

Then, one day, as every other day, the father slowly walks out to the front gate. But, today was going to be different. He saw a form in the distance. The father might have said, "Oh, are my eyes deceiving me? Could it be? Is that really my boy?" As the form turned into reality, the father exclaimed, "It's him! I've prayed every day for him to come home. I know it's him...I would recognize that walk and that face anywhere. It's my boy!"

4. *A father has forgiveness for his children.* "He ran to his son, threw his arms around him and kissed him" (Luke 15:20). Only Jesus could paint such a bold picture of a loving God who accepts His children when they return. The father *ran* to his son! Do you see it? What a picture of our heavenly Father. He ran! The God of the universe is pictured running with love to greet His boy returning home. Oh, what a Savior!

5. *A father has resources to share with his children.* "But the father said to his servants, 'Quick! Bring the best robe and put it on him. Put a ring on his finger and sandals on his feet. Bring the fattened calf and kill it. Let's have a feast and celebrate'" (Luke 15:22-23). All the resources the son ever needed for happiness and success is found at his father's house. When he went into the far country,

he got what he thought he wanted, but soon realized that it was not what was advertised. Instead of "eating off the menu" at the finest restaurants, he "became the menu" for a herd of pigs! His father had more than just natural resources to share with his wayward son who came home. Having a "welcome home" party is one thing, but receiving mercy and grace is an entirely different and wonderful matter.

6. *A father has a redemptive heart.* *"'My son,' the father said, 'you are always with me, and everything I have is yours. But we had to celebrate and be glad, because this brother of yours was dead and is alive again; he was lost and is found'"* (Luke 15:31). The message of this parable is one of redemption, grace, and a loving God who invites His children who may be wandering in the desert of discontentment to come back to the Father's house!

Though we reject him, God never rejects us! He lovingly awaits our coming to him—with arms wide open, longing to receive and restore to us, without hesitation.

—Dan Wierenga

By the way, the point of this parable includes daughters too!

GREAT LEADERS ARE GREAT THINKERS

Set your minds on things above, not on earthly things.

—COLOSSIANS 3:2

Let a man radically alter his thoughts, and he will be astonished at the rapid transformation it will affect in the material conditions of his life.

—JAMES ALLEN[1]

Introduction

Several years ago, an African-American university advertised extensively on the television. The tagline at the end of the commercial said, "A mind is a terrible thing to waste." No truer words have ever been spoken, especially if you have had the privilege of raising teenagers. How many times have we looked at our kids and muttered, "What in the world were they thinking?"

But, the failure to "think" is not just confined to teenagers. As we grow and mature, we tend to fall into the trap of believing that spending time thinking about the issues we face is a substitute for hard work. The mantra is, "Why waste time thinking about a problem, just get up and do something!"

According to Merriam-Webster, the definition of *thinking* is, "the action of using one's mind to produce thoughts." The mind is the most powerful muscle we possess, and like any muscle, it must constantly be engaged in an activity to reach its full potential. Neglecting the brain runs the risk of intellectual atrophy, just like ignoring the other muscle groups of your body. Strategic and purposeful thinking is an essential exercise of the brain that keeps you fresh with new and innovative ideas.

Glenn Davis observed:

> What is thinking? It is basically our mind talking to ourselves. Every human being is constantly talking to themselves—they just don't usually do it out loud. Everyone has both negative and positive fleeting thoughts. You know the kind. They just seem to come into our mind from nowhere. These are not the thoughts that will affect our destiny. If it is just in and out there is no lasting impression; but, if we choose to spend time dwelling or meditating about the thought, then it becomes a part of who we are and will impact our lives for better or worse.[2]

I have discovered there is a vast difference between successful leaders and those who claim some measure of success. What stands out to me is this: those who maintain success longer than others are willing to do those "unseemly" things that set them apart. Such things as: if necessary, work longer hours; refuse to take time off when deadlines are approaching; reject distractions that take them away from the goal; and, a willingness to risk their current level of success to go to a higher level.

A proverb says, *"For as he thinks in his heart, so is he"* (Proverbs 23:7 NKJV). That Proverb has been proven right for thousands of years. It is historically factual that you will act the same way you think. Actions will always follow beliefs, maybe not overnight, but they will eventually catch up. For instance, if you allow negative thoughts to dominate your mind, you will find a way to sabotage your success. If you think you will never have enough resources to get the job done, you probably won't; and, if you are always looking for the other shoe to drop, it likely will. You cannot run your business or your life always thinking the worst, because thinking your worst will never produce your best!

Fred Rogers, aka Mr. Rogers of PBS fame, was considered by many to be one of the great thinkers of his time. He revolutionized television for children, and his impact is still being felt today. The following is a brief description of a typical day in the life of Mr. Rogers.

> Don't doubt that Fred Rogers was indeed a great thinker, despite the fact that he is best known as the familiar Mr. Rogers from the long-lasting PBS children's show. His television show was a safe place for many young children, by his design, and he fought hard, in his quiet manner, for the show to stay on the air. The famous routine that started and ended his show was not the only routine in his life. Each day he would wake at 5:30 and begin his day with reading, writing, study, and prayer. He would take a swim most days of his life, take a late-afternoon nap, and go to bed at 9:30 each night. Perhaps the most idiosyncratic of his rituals was that he kept his weight at

143 pounds his entire adult life. He saw his weight one day and realized it aligned with the number of letters in "I love you" and vowed to maintain that weight, which he did.[3]

Author Elizabeth Fillppouli gave her perspective on the age-old question about leaders. She queried:

> Are leaders made or born? Let's for a moment forget the "talent" or the "high IQ" arguments. Studies have shown that neither is worth anything without motivation, guidance, encouragement and hard, hard and even harder work. You need to be ten times faster and work ten times harder to succeed as a leader. Leaders are made. They are the result of a never-ending process of self-study, education, training, and experience. Leadership is learned.[4]

Three Thinking Tools Every Leader Should Carry

There are three thinking tools every leader should carry daily if they are to fulfill their potential: a pair of binoculars, a laser beam, and a mirror. Let's look at each in detail.

1. A Pair of Binoculars

Short-term thinking is excellent for short-term issues, but to generate confidence in those we lead and to establish a foundation to build on, we must be willing to take a *long-term approach*. If we are going to produce a long-term strategy, we must be ready to pick up a pair of "mental binoculars" and see as far down the road as possible.

I'm not suggesting we ignore what is in front of us, but to realize it is not either/or, it is actually both/and when it comes to success.

What does long-term thinking look like?

- *Long-term thinking* involves developing a vision for where you see your ministry and/or business in the future. Where you want to go and how to get there requires two critical factors. *First*, your attitude, which is thinking; and *second*, your actions, which involve working. You can't have one without the other.

- *Long-term thinking* not only establishes a vision for the future, but with a clear vision comes a set of priorities that act as guardrails to keep the goals in view.

- *Long-term thinking* may require us to step into areas that are unfamiliar and hold a certain amount of risk. But to possess what we have never had may require doing something we have never done!

- *Long-term thinking* is also out of the box thinking. Your box may be different from mine, but any restrictions we put on ourselves will hinder the pursuit of our vision. Reject small-minded thinking and short-term success. If you are going to dream, you might as well dream big!

In 2019, Jeff Bezos was the richest man in the world. He did not arrive at such lofty heights by taking shortcuts and falling prey to quick fixes. We may never attain that title, but there is plenty to learn from a man who refused to neglect the process of long-term thinking.

Ali Rushdan, writing for Fastcompany.com said this about Bezos:

From Amazon's inception, Jeff Bezos has been clear about his long-term strategy. In fact, he frequently tells his loyal team that every day is Day One at the company, suggesting that they are in for the long-haul. This serves two purposes: 1. It develops long-term commitment to Amazon's goals, and 2. It protects the team against hasty short-term decisions. Together with the company's marshalling of large investments into projects, it's no wonder that Bezos and his team have caught the ire of investors looking for a quick return on their dollars. But Bezos has remained firm in his beliefs. Frustrating Wall Street quarter after quarter with slim profits, Amazon has gone about its business writing its own rules. And, ironically, to roaring success; since its inception, Amazon has returned its most patient investors with over 1,000% returns.[5]

2. A Laser Beam

A successful leader will not only look downstream but will pick up a laser beam and learn to focus on the most important objects that lead toward success. I'm talking about focused thinking. A very successful missionary, named Paul, said, *"In the same way, I run straight for the place at the end of the race. I fight to win. I do not beat the air"* (1 Corinthians 9:26 NLV).

The Roman philosopher and renowned thinker Seneca observed, "The archer must know what he is seeking to hit; then he must aim and control the weapon by his skill. Our plans miscarry because they have no aim. When a man does not know what harbor he is making for, no wind is the right wind."[6]

What will laser beam thinking do?

- *Laser beam thinking is guided thinking.* Your focus
  will be established in your daily routine. A daily to-do
  list is essential. It is a proven fact that daily goals are
  much more attainable when written down, rather
  than keeping them locked away in your mental filing
  cabinet. Your focus will be maintained when you
  attach a time frame for completion.

- *Laser beam thinking eliminates generalities.* Our military has perfected the "smart" bomb that can be
  directed to any target and hit it with amazing accu-
  racy. It is guided by a laser beam that can lock on a
  target from hundreds of miles away. We need to learn
  that when we practice laser-guided thinking, we will
  blot out whatever may be clamoring for our attention
  and focus on the priorities we have established.

- *Laser beam thinking requires time and effort.* Henry
  Ford said, "Thinking is the hardest work there is,
  which is probably the reason why so few engage in it."[7]

The following story illustrates the power of laser-guided thinking.

One day the Zen master wanted to show his students a
new technique of shooting an arrow. He told his students
to cover his eyes with a cloth and then he shot his arrow.
When he opened his eyes, he saw the target with no arrow
in it and when he looked at his students, they looked
embarrassed because their teacher had missed.

The Zen master asked them, "What lesson do you think
I intend to teach you all today?" They answered, "We

43

thought you would show us how to shoot at the target without looking." The Zen master said, "No, I taught you that if you want to be successful in life, don't forget the target. You have to keep an eye on the target, otherwise you may miss a good opportunity in life." They looked at each other, impressed with the lesson.

The moral of the story is we need to consistently focus on what we want and we need to realize that: What thoughts we focus on we FEEL; therefore, our thoughts have a direct effect on our emotions. What we focus on and feel we attract in our lives. Our destiny is consistently shaped by our thoughts.[8]

3. A Mirror

If I want to see what I really look like, it's best to look in a mirror and not a photograph. Why? A mirror will tell me the truth, warts and all, while a picture can be touched up to make me look better than I am. If I cut myself shaving, I don't grab a ten-year-old photograph to look at my face. How silly. No, I go to the mirror to give myself an accurate assessment.

Columnist Geoff Masters wrote an article titled "Learning from Mistakes." In it he wrote:

> A willingness to acknowledge and learn from failure is essential for all progress. Obstacles to acknowledging mistakes include the desire to protect personal reputations and deeply held beliefs. However, when evidence is avoided, hidden or ignored, learning opportunities are lost. This is true at the level of individuals and is equally true at the level of organizations, industries and professions.[9]

Everyone has made mistakes and experienced failure. Yes, all of us, no exceptions. A smart leader will spend time not rehashing the past, but will make every effort to reflect and learn from past experiences to avoid the same mistakes in the future. There is nothing wrong with correcting what went wrong, but we cannot live in the land of "I wish I had not done that" for very long. Nothing will stifle present and future growth more than always looking in the rearview mirror. There comes the point when we need to pull up the anchor of past mistakes and set our sails with the wind of progress for the future!

What will mirror thinking do?

- *Mirror thinking separates fact from fiction.* Realistic thinking is the opposite of wishful thinking. Just because people take an honest look at their situation does not mean they have given up hope that things will change for the better. When I apply realism to my situation, I am then moved out of the land of "wishing and hoping" things will change into a land of "I can make this happen if I make an honest assessment of my situation." Mirror thinking is not either/or, it's both/and.

- *Mirror thinking will keep me grounded.* I have learned the hard way that making emotional decisions will take me to a place I don't want to go. I have to remind myself that while I reach for the stars, I need to keep my feet planted solidly on the ground. Mirror thinking forces me to analyze each situation with a critical eye.

- *Mirror thinking is NOT negative thinking.* I am by nature a positive thinker. But I must confess there are times when I slip into a negative mindset that has the potential to overwhelm my positivity. I have learned the value of replacing all negative self-talk with a realistic view.

James Allen observed, "A particular train of thought persisted in, be it good or bad, cannot fail to produce its results on the character and circumstances. A man cannot directly choose his circumstances, but he can choose his thoughts, and so indirectly, yet surely, shape his circumstances."[10]

Three Common Characteristics of Great Thinkers

While it's true that no two sets of fingerprints are alike, it's also true that no two leaders are alike. Except for one thing. How they think. Leader who know how to unlock the power that's between their ears have a far better opportunity for success than those who only use their heads as hat racks.

1. *Great thinkers recognize that thinking is an asset, not a liability.*

I read an article by Brian Scudamore that said Warren Buffett spent 80 percent of his career reading and thinking. Buffett, CEO of the largest public company in the United States in 2018, Berkshire Hathaway, doesn't feel that spending time "thinking" is a waste of time. On the contrary, says Charlie Munger, Buffett's long-time business partner, "That's what created [one of the] world's most successful business records in history. He has a lot of time to think."[11]

Scudamore goes on the explain: "Buffett's schedule may seem like an anomaly. In reality, he's a trailblazer. Thanks in part to his example, over the past few years several high-profile CEOs have come out against the norm of constant busyness. They argue that critical thinking time is essential in a complex, rapidly changing digital economy."[12]

What about you? Look at your schedule. Do you have a time built in just to think? Have you fallen victim to the traditional approach to success that says you have to work your fingers to the bone and sacrifice family, friends, and health to achieve a measure of success?

2. *Great thinkers are not afraid to ask, "Why?"*

Curiosity may have killed the cat, but a common trait among the world's greatest thinkers is their inquisitive nature. Strategic thinking and curiosity seem to go hand in hand. It was this kind of thinking that led to some of the world's greatest inventions.

I share just two of many:

A Household Invention by Earle Dickson

Earle Dickson was employed as a cotton buyer for the Johnson & Johnson when he invented the Band-Aid in 1921 for his wife Josephine Dickson, who was always cutting her fingers in the kitchen while preparing food.

At that time a bandage consisted of separate gauze and adhesive tape that you would cut to size and apply yourself, but Earle Dickson noticed that gauze and adhesive tape she used would soon fall off her active fingers, and he decided to invent something that would stay in place and protect small wounds better.

Earle Dickson took a piece of gauze and attached it to the center of a piece of tape then covered the product with crinoline to keep it sterile. This ready-to-go product allowed his wife to dress her wounds without assistance, and when Earle's boss James Johnson saw the invention, he decided to manufacture band-aids to the public and make Earle Dickson vice-president of the company.[13]

Earmuffs: "Baby It's Cold Outside!"

"Baby, It's Cold Outside" may have been the song running through 13-year-old Chester Greenwood's head one cold December day in 1873. To protect his ears while ice skating, he found a piece of wire, and with his grandmother's help, padded the ends.

In the beginning, his friends laughed at him. However, when they realized that he was able to stay outside skating long after they had gone inside freezing, they stopped laughing. Instead, they began to ask Chester to make ear covers for them, too. At age 17 Chester applied for a patent. For the next 60 years, Chester's factory made earmuffs, and earmuffs made Chester rich.[14]

3. *Great thinkers are lifelong learners.*

I learned a long time ago that I don't have to have the answers to everything. As a matter of fact, the older I get, the more I realize how little I know about life's mysteries. But, I made up my mind that just because I don't know everything that should not stop me from trying to learn something new every day I am left on this planet.

I have the privilege to work alongside some brilliant people. But, I have never met a man or woman who had the answers to everything.

Happy was the day when I decided to use three little words that changed my thinking forever: *"I don't know!"* To admit not knowing something was a quick motivation that moved me to dig and find the answer. If you want to become a great thinker, then become a lifelong learner. It's okay to say, "I don't know," especially when you *really* don't know.

> Great thinkers are great learners. Those that listen proactively, strategically and intuitively are often more capable of putting in place strategies and plans that address challenges head-on with a big impact.
>
> —RICHARD BRANSON

A Final Thought

Don't ever allow anyone to convince you that using your brain to think is a waste of time or your talent. It's not! If you want to stand out in a crowd, you must be willing to do what the crowd refuses to do.

Author Mark Morgan Ford summed it up for me when he wrote:

To be a great thinker, you must be willing to:

- spend some serious time noodling over life's important questions
- reject any idea that comes to you prepackaged
- discover the principles in play behind big ideas
- be rigorous in testing your ideas against your experience

And most of all, you must be brave enough to voice opinions that aren't popular. After all, if independent thinking means anything, it means thinking thoughts that differ from those of the mainstream.[15]

4

GREAT LEADERS SEE THINGS THAT DON'T SEEM TO EXIST

Then the Lord replied: "Write down the revelation and make it plain on tablets so that a herald may run with it."
—HABAKKUK 2:2

Vision without action is a daydream. Action without vision is a nightmare.
—JAPANESE PROVERB[1]

Introduction

It is an undeniable fact that many who hold positions of leadership operate without any sense of direction or an established vision for the future. Trying to lead an organization without a vision is like trying to steer a car without a steering wheel. It may look like a car, but the last thing you want to do is take it out on the interstate and try to maneuver through traffic.

A friend shared with me the following account that illustrates what many organizations look like without a functioning visionary leader:

> I had just boarded my flight out of Meridian, Mississippi. I had to make a connection in Atlanta, Georgia. It was one of those small puddle-jumpers that only seated 10 or 12 passengers. As we were about to depart, the pilot made an announcement. He said that our flight had been held up because of heavy air traffic at the Atlanta airport. The pilot also said that since we were already on the tarmac, there was no need to deplane. We just needed to be patient; it would not be long before we would be on our way.
>
> Suddenly, after about an hour wait, the engines roared to life and everyone cheered thinking we were about to take off. But, that was not to be. What the pilot did next was hysterical. He taxied the plane to the end of the tarmac, leading to the main runway, turned around and taxied back to where we started. We made at least four roundtrips. When the pilot heard everyone laughing, he announced that he thought it would a good way to kill time and give us some free sightseeing.
>
> I thought to myself, "No matter how many times we circle the runway in Meridian, Mississippi, we are never going to land at the Atlanta airport. At some point, we have to take off!"

When he told me that story, it reminded me of organizations that never seem to "take off" because of a lack of vision. I am convinced that no organization can last very long without a defined vision that is well thought out and executed by a visionary leader. Visionary leadership is not an option—it is a requirement to affect change for changing times. Without visionary leadership, the organization will become nothing more than a puddle-jumper sightseeing around the economic landscape.

How Do You Measure Success?

Is success measured by the size of your bank account?

Money is not the root of all evil. The Bible says, *"For the love of money is a root of all kinds of evil, for which some have strayed from the faith in their greediness, and pierced themselves through with many "sorrows"* (1 Timothy 6:10 NKJV).

It is the love of money that causes people to forfeit their families, friends, and shipwreck their companies. Some people believe that if they can accumulate wealth, they will be successful. Wealth in itself is not evil—nor is it the answer to peace, contentment, or success.

Is success based on how happy you are?

Plenty of books have been written around the theme of "If something makes you happy," then you are a successful person. In other words, if you feel successful, you will be successful. The continual search for happiness is a primary factor in the misery index of so many people. Life is full of ups and downs, good days, and bad days. No one is exempt from the sunshine or the rain; it falls on all of us. If happiness is your "goal," then you will stay on a roller coaster of emotions all of your life.

Is success achieving goals?

Having goals is a good thing. But merely reaching a particular goal is not a substitute for a vision for the future. If we are not careful, we can get so focused on our daily to-do list that we miss the big picture. One of my goals in life is to make certain *all* my goals have future goals.

Is success MORE than just acquiring wealth, power, fame, and feeling good?

YES! It is so much more than all that because success is not found in any one thing. Success is found in a person's knowledge of why he or she was put on planet Earth, and a willingness to maximize the person's potential. You hold the key to your future. What you do with that key is entirely up to you. Each of us has a key called "potential." But if you don't use it to unlock your vision, then it becomes nothing more than a reminder of what could have been.

> Success is not being in the right place at the right time, but being the right person all the time.
> —UNKNOWN AUTHOR

I have a question: Are you willing to take the necessary steps to unlock your potential? I don't believe that people start out with the idea of not seeing their vision fulfilled. Defining what you want and where you want to go with your life is crucial. If you don't know the answer, it is impossible to share the necessary information you need for a successful leadership journey. Life is a marathon, not a sprint.

> Strategic planning in any company begins with the company's vision. The vision is where the company sees itself in the future—where it wants to be and how it wants to be known.
> —WILLIAM DOUGLAS and RUBENS TEIXEIRA[2]

You Might Be a Visionary Leader *IF*...

1. ...*You are willing to change what is not working.*

Many so-called leaders refuse to change things that are no longer working because, to them, it is a sign of failure. I don't know too many people who like to change, because change represents a disruption in the way things have always been done.

A visionary leader has learned to recognize that for any enterprise to succeed, it takes a commitment and a plan of action to produce positive change. Introducing positive change will include a new and better-defined vision, one that may incorporate elements of the old but will reshape the vision to meet modern demands.

> By definition, a vision is a concept that is not yet real. The first step in formulating a vision is to simply start thinking about what could be rather than what presently exists. This does take a certain amount of optimism; the critical and skeptical will seldom have visions or dreams.
>
> —RICK JOYNER[3]

It is never easy to undertake change. Whether we like it or not, change is part of life. No matter how hard we try, we can't stop the waves of change washing over us. If we don't handle change properly, a strong reaction will shake the foundation of our organization, much like an earthquake. Once we understand that change is inevitable, our thinking becomes, *How will we handle change when it happens?*

A visionary leader must be willing to deal with various reactions when introducing change. Whether it's eliminating processes that are not working, retooling policies that need updating, or launching an entirely new product, there will always be a reaction from those involved. So a visionary leader must be prepared.

Burt Nanus observed the following about introducing change:

> The key to gaining widespread commitment to a new vision, therefore, is to present a vision in such a way that people will want to participate and will freely choose to do so. This certainly cannot be done through coercion or manipulation, for people must freely and enthusiastically accept the vision or they will not have the energy or excitement to work for its fulfillment. Besides, the use of coercion or manipulation implies a cynical belief that people are reluctant participants in the work of the organization. The only approach that will work is based on exactly the opposite belief—that people are interested in active partners and colleagues in the enterprise—and involves discussing the vision with them in terms that address their own legitimate concerns and interests.[4]

Three Most Common Roadblocks to Change

One. Fear of the unknown. I have found that most people are open to change when it comes to better ways of doing things things. But at some level, fear affects everyone, it's just part of life. If I allow my fear to become greater than my desire to change things for the better, I will never realize my dreams or reach my goals. But don't make changes if it's working. Change just for change sake is a disaster. If it isn't broken, don't try and fix it.

Two. Negative attitude. A negative attitude can manifest itself in many ways. The most common is the attitude expressed when people are asked why they are against change: "I just like the old way better!"

Dealing with negativity is one of the most challenging aspects of being a leader. Let's face it, a negative person will find something to be disappointed about no matter what we do.

Three. Fear of failure. Tradition and the "old ways of doing things" is a change killer. Even if something is no longer producing results, some people will hold on like grim death. Why? Because attempting something new usually leads into unchartered territory and there is always the possibility of failure.

2. ...You can maintain your priorities.

Setting and maintaining priorities may be one of the most difficult tasks a visionary leader faces. We are living in an age of instant communication—smart phones and hundreds of other devices— that demand our attention. Sadly, many leaders are tied to their devices. They will respond to the beep of a text, email, or voicemail even if it interrupts family time or date night with their spouse. The urgent sounds of a smart phone have replaced the vital pleadings of issues and people who are far more important!

3. ...You are willing to take responsibility for the wins as well as the losses.

More than one leader has been stopped dead in their tracks by playing the blame game. If, as the old leadership proverb says, "Everything rises and falls on leadership," then by accepting that definition, we must take responsibility for losses as well as wins. You can't have it both ways—blaming others for failures, and accepting all the praise for success. Sadly, it has become easier to avoid responsibility at all costs rather than take responsibility no matter the cost!

Ron Bliwas, writing *in The C Student's Guide to Success,* states:

People who are known for taking responsibility seriously aren't always the best and the brightest, but they are the ones every boss wants on her team. Responsible people are much more likely to receive promotions and attract and keep customers than people with technical or other organizational skills. There is no substitute for the person who is completely reliable and dogged in the pursuit of her goals. Many people pay lip service to being responsible, but they don't take their responsibilities seriously. You've probably heard a professional coach or athlete say that he takes complete responsibility for a loss, but you never believe for a minute that he is going to lose a minute's worth of sleep—or a dollar's worth of income—over the loss.[5]

According to Merriam-Webster.com, *responsibility* is defined as the quality or state of being responsible: something for which one is responsible. And according to Blanche Brick, PhD, "We demand corporate responsibility for a shoddy product or a polluted beach, however, we refused to require individuals to except responsibility for their acts of irresponsible behavior. Perhaps it is easier to legislate and regulate spoiled meat than it is to legislate or regulate spoiled people—whether they are from the west side of Chicago or the president of a savings and loan."[6]

Three P's of Responsibility

One. Practicing—what you believe. The foundation of all of our choices and actions are based on our core principles. Knowing what we believe and acting accordingly determines our success in every area of life. It is a fact of life that wrong belief structures will lead to a faulty foundation that will crack under the pressure of intense scrutiny.

Two. Placing—goals that are challenging. The One who created you has put within you certain dreams and ambitions, as well as the ability to overcome any challenges you might face. Getting to where you want to go requires the discipline of setting and reaching your goals. Several years ago, a man climbed to the top of Mount Everest. Nothing unusual about that, hundreds have accomplished the same thing; except this man is blind! His name is Erik Weihenmayer, and he reached the summit on May 25, 2001. Oh, and by the way, he also climbed to the top of Mount Ararat—and completed the Seven Summits climb in September 2002.[7]

Three. Persisting—until the job is finished. Winning always comes on the heels of those who don't give up; it's called persistence. Staying with the task has enabled many people to claim great success. It's incredible how much "luck" people have who are inspired. Why? They found the secret of creating their inspiration and how to motivate themselves to reach seemingly impossible goals. The Bible tells us that you will always reap what you sow (Galatians 6:7). Remember, "The only things in life that do not require discipline are bad habits."

Thomas Edison once explained the vast majority of his patents and inventions were someone else's—he was just the one who finished what another had started. Edison understood the importance of discipline in everything he did, whether it was considered important or trivial.

Responsibility also carries the idea of finishing what you start. Each time we fulfill a responsibility, there comes with it peace and contentment that is rewarding and personally satisfying. An old

Chinese proverb says, "The end of a thing is greater than its beginning." I think that means, how you finish is more important than how you start.

> Parties who want milk should not seat themselves on a stool in the middle of the field in hope that the cow will back up to them.
>
> —ELBERT HUBBARD

4. ...You can break free from procrastination.

According to Webster's dictionary, *procrastination* is a verb that means to be slow or late about doing something that should be done; to delay doing something until a later time because you did not want to do it, or because you are lazy, etc. In other words, procrastination is a slow death by a thousand cuts; or more accurately, it is putting off until tomorrow what should have been done yesterday!

Clean off your desk! Just because you have a cluttered desk and your inbox is running over does not necessarily mean you are important, or busy. Your desk may be nothing more than a silent reminder that there are things that need to be done, but you are stuck in the endless cycle of procrastination.

I read the following account about Benjamin S. Bull, the founder of the Medal Gold Flower Company.

> During a meeting with the company's top managers, Bull asked a high-ranking officer to report on the status of one of Bull's pet projects. The manager said his department had not gotten around to working on the project, but they would attend to it eventually. Bull was an impatient man, and in exasperation, he jumped up from the meeting table, leaned over the startled manager and shouted,

"Eventually? Why not now?" The expression *"Eventually? Why not now?"* made such a profound impact on the Medal Gold management team that it was immediately adopted as the company's motto—and it remained the Medal Gold motto for more than 50 years![8]

The moral of the story: there is always something we can do to move us toward our objective. Instead of staring at that mountain of paperwork and unfinished tasks, why not pick up one single assignment and get busy.

Take control of your time. The list of excuses as to why we don't get things done is endless. One of my favorites is, "I don't have enough time." Not being able to control our time is a discipline flaw that comes from the root of procrastination. In most cases, we *can* control the events of our lives, notwithstanding the unexpected things, like rushing out the door for an urgent appointment only to discover you have a flat tire.

Todd Duncan writes:

> Time waits for no one. We cannot blockade it. We cannot stall it. It is like a rushing torrent that demands we deal with it, work with it, and use it. It is an ongoing continuum of events that have happened, are happening, or will happen in the future. Our success in the game of life comes from how we merge the activities and events that we say are important into a planned time to execute them. That is why executives are called executives, but we do not need a corner window with a view of the city to be an executive. When we learn to merge our activities into a planned time for execution, we become executives. We

receive immediate feedback—like stepping on a rake—because we know immediately whether we are living on purpose or by accident. It is always our choice.[9]

Why not today? One of the most popular reasons people give for procrastination is they think all tasks have to be completed in one day. Most of the time, having to finish something in one day is because we have put it off for so long it has now become an emergency. The key is taking small steps, which will keep us from becoming overwhelmed. Never file your procrastination under the heading of, "I work harder when things reach a boiling point!"

Earl Nightingale said, "The Chinese have a saying that a journey of a thousand miles begins with but a single step. And that step accomplishes two things. First, it automatically shortens the distance we still have to travel, and, second, and just as important, it makes us feel better, more hopeful—it strengthens our faith.[10]

5. ...You are willing to share your vision with others.

Proverbs 29:18 says, *"Where there is no revelation, people cast off restraint; but blessed is the one who heeds wisdom's instruction."*

The King James Version's phrase is *"Where there is no vision, the people perish,"* which means to "cast off restraint," or better yet, "to live without any sense of direction. It is a picture of a horse without a bit and bridle." That is why visionary leadership is so vital to any group, business organization, or church.

The dreamers are the saviors of the world. As the visible world is sustained by the invisible, so men, through all their trials and sins and sordid vocations, are nourished by the beautiful visions of their solitary dreamers. Humanity cannot forget its dreamers. It cannot let their ideals fade and die. It lives in them. It knows them in the realities which it shall one day see and know.[11]

What Happens When You Share Your Vision?

Your vision will create excitement. Sharing your vision with others has the potential to create a "buzz" much like touching an electrified "live wire." It will stimulate and release a dynamitic creativity; and before you know it, others who may have been initially skeptical will join the parade. I have seen more than once when the vision is shared, a creative force sweeps through the organization.

Your vision will create a new commitment. If the vision is right, those who have been looking and longing for a new direction will do everything possible to make it become a reality. By and large, people want to buy into a new and exciting vision, and they will find ways to brainstorm and make it even bigger and better.

Your vision will create lasting change. The religious world is a great source of illustrations about the importance of imparting vision. If you know anything about the church world, you know the resistance to anything new, such as a new vision, is monumental.

Leith Anderson tells the following story in his excellent book, *Dying for Change:*

> The church was desperate. Years of decline had taken a painful toll. "What we need," they said, "is a dynamic new pastor."
>
> A blue-ribbon search committee did everything right to find the perfect leader. He was young but experienced, serious but witty, articulate but not intimidating, spiritual but worldly wise. If anyone could turn this problem-ridden congregation around, he was the man.

When the pastoral candidate first addressed the congregation, he gave an inspiring description of his qualifications, experience, vision, and plans. His final line summed up his stirring presentation: "With God's help, I intend to lead this church forward into the nineteenth century!"

Surprised and embarrassed by the candidate's apparent mistake, the chairman of the search committee whispered loudly, "You mean the twentieth century!"

To which the candidate replied, "We're going to take this one century at a time!"[12]

A Final Thought

The ability for visionary leaders to "see" what is ahead and plan accordingly does not make them better or smarter, just different. Imparting a vision is not reserved for a few mystics or spooky people who have lost touch with reality. A visionary leader is someone willing to invest the time and energy into seeing the organization become the best it can be.

One such man was Allen Neuharth, CEO of the Gannett Company:

> When he launched the *USA Today* national newspaper 25 [years] ago, Allen Neuharth, the CEO of Gannett Company from 1973-1986, was derided by both Wall Street analysts and the newspaper establishment. Having built a very successful chain of regional newspapers and having been named the newspaper publishing Chief Executive of the Year by the *Wall Street Transcript* in 1979, why would Neuharth want to take such a bold and seemingly foolish

risk? Who would buy "bite-size" news? The answer today is clear—millions would buy it and continue to buy it, but that was certainly not the case in 1982 when the paper was launched. Neuharth saw a future for his family's newspaper empire that others could not see. He also saw a time-starved consumer base that was thirsty for news in manageable chunks. Capitalizing on his regional network of newspaper organizations, Neuharth created an elaborate logistical process to produce and deliver a national newspaper to supplement, not replace, regional carriers. What was it about Neuharth that enabled him to see the vast possibilities of a national newspaper? He clearly possessed a vision of what could be and more importantly, the ability to make it a reality.[13]

5

GREAT LEADERS ARE NOT AFRAID OF HARD WORK

Whatever your hand finds to do, do it with all your might, for in the realm of the dead, where you are going, there is neither working nor planning nor knowledge nor wisdom.

—ECCLESIASTES 9:10

I don't pity any man who does hard work worth doing. I admire him. I pity the creature who does not work, at whichever end of the social scale he may regard himself as being.

—THEODORE ROOSEVELT[1]

Introduction

I don't know anyone who starts out to be a failure. Whether launching a new business or rebranding an old one, the idea of "going under" never flashes across their minds. Unfortunately, failures do occur, and things that started with a bang often end up in a fizzle. There usually isn't just one reason why things don't work out the way we think they should. But in many cases, it could boil down to a false view of the meaning of work.

Some people view work as a means of building up their bank account. While it is true that money is essential, and we need it to function in our culture, it is only part of the whole package. For instance, if money alone was all it took to be successful, then why do so many rich and famous people commit suicide? No one will ever know all the reasons why someone decides to take their own life, but in many cases, it had nothing to do with money.

> Our definition of success is unorthodox. We claim that any man who is honest, fair, tolerant, kindly, charitable of others and well behaved is a success, no matter what his station in life.
>
> —JAY E. HOUSE[2]

Many people believe that King Solomon was the richest man who ever lived. This man had it all. He had more power and money than we can possibly imagine. And yet when he came to the end of his life, he offered insight on the matter, *"Let us hear the conclusion of the whole matter: Fear God, and keep his commandments: for this is the whole duty of man. For God shall bring every work into judgment, with every secret thing, whether it be good, or whether it be evil"* (Ecclesiastes 12:13-14 King James Version). And work is good, as long as it's the right kind!

We are living in a culture that seeks to avoid work. For some, the modern-day motto is, "How little can we do and still do all the things we want to do?" I am not suggesting that we work twenty-four hours a day, seven days a week, that would be silly. We all need time to rest, reflect, and refresh.

If we choose to see the obstacles in our path as barriers, we stop trying. If we choose to see the obstacles as hurdles, we can leap over them. Successful people don't have fewer problems. They have determined that nothing will stop them from going forward.

—BEN CARSON[3]

If we ever want to rise above the level of mediocrity, we must remember it doesn't happen accidentally. It means there comes a time when we combine our words with our actions, which will in turn produce the desired results. As mentioned previously, the adage our parents used to say, *"Don't do as I do, but do as I say,"* is no longer valid. Our *saying* and our *doing* must be in harmony!

Many uninformed people think that work is an ancient curse. As you study the Bible, you find that God was the Source of creation; therefore, He was the first worker. Someone said God worked so hard He had to rest on the seventh day! Since God never changes, work is still a priority with Him. If the Lord had been a dreamer and never followed up with action, the earth would still be in His mind, and we would not be on it. Everything around us is a product of hard work.

Let's face it—everyone has great ideas, dreams, and goals in the shower. Some of my best strategies have happened in that solitary place. But I learned that to be a successful leader, I needed to dry off, put on my clothes, and get to work. Author David Bly observed, "Striving for success without hard work is like trying to harvest where you haven't planted."[4] I could not agree more!

You do not come across success just by hoping for it. To achieve true success, you need the strength of mind and body to struggle and work hard to reach your fullest potential. You need the right attitude, self-discipline and the ability to put your goal before your own needs, if you are really driven towards reaching success.

—ANDREI U[5]

Three Character Traits of Leaders Who Stop Talking and Start Doing

1. *Great leaders develop habits that lead to success.*

The definition of *habit* in Webster's New World Dictionary is "a habit is an acquired pattern of action that is so automatic it's difficult to break; a thing done often and hence, usually, done easily; practice; custom."

You notice the definition does not indicate whether a habit is good or bad. Habits exist in all of us—some are positive and some are negative, but we all have them.

Burke Hedges, in his book titled *You, Inc.,* observed:

> Unfortunately, for most people, the word habit has a negative connotation, mainly because we've been conditioned to concentrate on the "difficult to break" part of the definition. That's what we think of when we use phrases like "smoking habit"…"drinking habit"…"drug habit"…and "habitual offender." But we need to remind ourselves that habits don't have to be bad or unproductive. It's obvious that people who acquire productive habits are far more likely to become successful…and fulfilled…and in control…than people who acquire unproductive habits.[6]

Let's be honest, as we mature, some changes take place rather easily while other areas of our life can be much more difficult to change, especially in the area of our habits.

When it comes to habits, I am reminded of a favorite Bible passage that is often quoted but seldom observed:

> *Do not be deceived: God cannot be mocked. A man reaps what he sows. Whoever sows to please their flesh, from the flesh will reap destruction; whoever sows to please the Spirit, from the Spirit will reap eternal life* (Galatians 6:7-8 NIV).

What that passage says to me is whatever habits we have sown is exactly what we will harvest.

It is foolish to think that a bad habit will ever produce a positive result. On the other hand, a productive habit, more often than not, will lead to a positive outcome. The choice is up to us as to which result we desire.

> What you're doing daily is determining what you're becoming permanently.
>
> —AUTHOR UNKNOWN

The simple truth is, your habits determine your destiny. Your daily routine is moving you toward or away from your desired future. The secret ingredient that maximizes and values time and minimizes mistakes is a successful routine based on productive habits. A successful routine is the result of right repeated actions, or the right habits. A very wise man, F. Matthias Alexander, said, "People do not decide their futures; they decide their habits and their habits decide their futures."

Once you decide to control your habits, you will gain control of your:

- Finances, including your spending habits
- Health, including a healthy lifestyle
- Time, including better time management
- Relationships, including placing value on those that are a priority

In other words, once you gain control of your habits, you will gain control of your life. It is helpful to remember that whatever you make a habit of is what you become. If you make a habit of winning, you are a winner. If you make a habit of giving, you are a giver. If you make a habit of learning something new every day, you become a life-long learner. Contrariwise, if you make a habit of losing, you will always end up wondering why you never see success.

> The diminutive chains of habit are seldom heavy enough to be felt, till they are too strong to be broken.
> —SAMUEL JOHNSON[7]

One of the best examples to understand how our habits shape our future is from a picture on the front of a Baptist Missions magazine. A friend of mine told me about the photograph. He said on the cover was a picture of a couple standing in front of their SUV. From the caption on the cover, they were somewhere in the remote expanse north of Fairbanks, Alaska. In the picture, there was a sign posted behind them that read, "Choose your rut carefully. You'll be in one for the next one hundred miles!"

Habits, like those ruts in Northern Alaska, are easy to fall into and yet according to the sign, *you better choose carefully,* because once you get in one, it's very tough to get out!

The real questions are: 1) Can habits be changed? 2) Are there ways to break a "bad" habit, and replace it with a "good" habit? Yes and yes! But only if the desire to change is greater than the desire to hang on to unproductive habits. Just by saying "I want to stop doing _____" (fill in the blank) doesn't mean you will. When it comes to changing liabilities into assets, it is time to *stop talking and start doing!*

I have spent a considerable amount of time reading and researching the most effective way to break bad habits. There are dozens of books on the bookshelf, and hundreds of articles on the Internet that offer sound advice on the best way to get it done. For me, simple is always better. So with that said, the following is the process that I have used successfully:

Make a list. Write down *all* habits, including the good, the bad, and the ugly. By using this simple first step, we can determine which ones should stay, which need to go, and which need to be improved.

Examples:

- A bad habit might be wasting too much time playing games on the computer or stopping at a drive-through for a quick snack on the way home after work.
- A good habit might be carving out time every day to invest in your future or developing a plan to spend time with family.

You get the point—make a list and be honest with yourself. Decide which habit needs to go into which category, then act accordingly.

Make a change. If you have ever tried to break free from a bad habit, you know how difficult it can be. Taking the first step to make a change may be hard, but until we are willing to jump into the deep end of the pool, nothing will ever change.

Instead of focusing attention on how unproductive or harmful a habit may be, why not change your thinking. If what you have been doing has not worked, why not change your traditional mindset to another point of view? How? Try thinking about the positive, instead of the negative.

Let's be real; if breaking bad habits were easy, then none of us would have any!

Examples:

- Bad habit: addicted to your smart phone.
- Positive habit replacement: Instead of cursing your cell phone, think about what you could do with the time wasted looking at all your social media accounts. How many walks could you take? How many books could you read? How much time have you missed interacting with family and friends?

Robert Taibbi wrote in *Psychology Today:* "Breaking habits isn't about stopping but substituting. Here is where you come up with a plan for managing the party without drinking—getting a mocktail and hanging close by your good friend, rather than grabbing a drink and being stuck with a bunch of strangers."[8]

Make an allowance. There may be times when we take three steps forward and four steps back. No one is immune from slipping up and walking right back into the same old habit pattern that we so proudly announced was finally broken. Instead of beating yourself up, recognize what happened, and start again tomorrow. More than likely, the habit that you despise didn't begin overnight and more than likely it won't be broken overnight either!

Habits don't form easily according to a scientific study published in the *European Journal of Social Psychology*. The study called How Long it Really Takes to Build a New Habit was headed by Dr. Phillippa Lally. She and her research team discovered that "On average, it takes more than 2 months before a new behavior becomes automatic—66 days to be exact. And how long it takes a new habit to form can vary widely depending on the behavior, the person, and the circumstances." In Lally's study, it took anywhere from 18 days to 254 days for people to form a new habit.[9]

The bottom line? Keep at it, and don't give up!

2. Great leaders keep their emotions under control.

Another quality trait of successful leaders is the ability to keep their emotions under control. Keeping our emotions in check is not the same as saying we should never allow our emotions to be seen. There is a big difference between keeping emotions in a lockbox and keeping our emotions in check. Keeping our feelings locked up until we explode in a fit of uncontrolled rage is not what I mean. We were not created to be robots or wander mindlessly through life. Emotions are good and necessary. They were given to us by our Creator.

On the flip side, the negative power of unchecked emotions is seen every day. You can't turn on the television without seeing our world is on fire with raging emotions. From your house to the White House, decisions are made daily, not based on reason and logic, but emotions. Wars have started and lives have been destroyed simply because something is done or said that raised the emotional level to fever pitch.

Our emotions are the driving powers of our lives. When we are aroused emotionally, unless we do something great and good, we are in danger of letting our emotions become perverted. William James used to tell the story of a Russian woman who sat weeping at the tragic fate of the hero in the opera while her coachman froze to death outside.

—EARL RINEY[10]

As far as going to work every day, let's face it, no one wants to be around a boss who is constantly riding on an emotional roller coaster. Taking the entire organization for a thrill ride of "I never know what he/she is going to be like today" leads to what I call the DISC of improper management:

D—Drains passion and creativity

I—Inconsistency is created

S—Saps the strength to go the extra mile

C— Clouds the focus of the organization

Keeping our emotions in check does not mean we never react to a situation. But it does mean that when faced with a decision or a course of action, we stop and gain a proper perspective on the situation.

Humans exhibit many facets of emotional range including fear, worry, pride, jealousy, and self-pity. But from the standpoint of leadership, there is one fruit from the root of the emotional tree that when left unchecked causes more harm and destruction than the rest put together—ANGER. When you couple anger along with its cousins bitterness, offense, wrath, and unforgiveness, you've got a powder keg ready to blow up your organization!

Speaking to a contestant on his game show, *You Bet Your Life,* Groucho Marx quipped: "If you speak when angry, you'll make the best speech you'll ever regret."[11] Anger, left to itself, can destroy personal happiness, kill relationships, and cause undue hardships for a moment or a lifetime.

Turn on any newscast today or pick up a newspaper and you can read about:

- Someone "going postal"—walking into a place of employment, angry over a perceived injustice and killing as many people as possible.

- A man driving an SUV, pursued by a gang of motorcyclists, being pulled from his car and beaten in front of his wife and child on a busy highway outside of New York City.

- A mother drowning her infant because she was irritated by the child's constant crying.

The examples of explosive and destructive anger are too many to list here—pick up your morning newspaper or open your favorite news website and read for yourself!

A *USA Today* survey revealed that 75 percent of Americans believe that angry behavior has increased in places such as airports and highways. Flight attendants and pilots report the dramatic increase in violent behavior among passengers. For example, in 1997 there were only 66 incidents of "air rage" reported; a short two years later, there were 534 incidents.

The physical effects of anger are both immediate and long term. God did not build the human body to handle anger without consequences. It is true an argument can be made that anger has its benefits such as warning that something inside is not right and it can move us out of apathy to accomplish and achieve great things. We must be very careful, though, trying to justify something that causes destructive behavior and untold misery.

How can we manage and keep our anger in check?

Walk, don't run. There is a recurring theme found in the book of Proverbs. The "wisdom" writer encouraged us to be slow to anger. Maybe that is why we have two ears and only one mouth—so we should listen twice as much as we talk! Sometimes the best way to stop the atomic explosion of rage is to stop talking and remove yourself physically from the detonator—the source of your anger.

Investigate before you castigate. Most of the time, anger is our natural response to perceived injustice. Many, if not most, issues would be resolved if we would stop long enough to identify the specific issues that our offender has committed. If we stop long enough to investigate, we may realize that our anger is unjustified and is based on false information, inaccurate facts, or indefensible assumptions.

Don't drink the poison. I have heard it said that anger directed toward others for a perceived hurt is like drinking poison and hoping the other person dies. If we are looking for things to upset us and make us angry, we probably won't have to look very far. Whether it's showing up on time for a doctor's appointment only to be told that the doctor is going to be two hours late; or picking up a to-go order at your favorite eatery, only to discover when you get home the order they gave you belonged to someone else. The list is endless of what can make us angry.

It is possible to make a conscious decision to overlook perceived injustices or hurt knowing that by doing so we are helping ourselves.

A wise person will see the difference between a minor offense and a major issue that must be resolved.

Comedian Buddy Hackett observed this about grudges: "I've had my share of disagreements in life, but I've learned never to carry a grudge, because while I'm carrying the grudge, the other person is out dancing."[12]

Chose to forgive. Not all offenses are based on false information; sometimes, they are genuine. It could be the result of a painful divorce, an abusive childhood, or an undeserved termination. The pain is real, and the injury hurts. God, in His wisdom, has given us a surgical procedure to heal the significant wounds we suffer—forgiveness.

Forgiveness is not approving or agreeing that the injury is justified. Forgiveness is not synonymous with denying or even minimizing the hurt. On the contrary, just as Joseph forgave his brothers for selling him into slavery, he did not ignore their injustice or sweep it under the rug. Instead, he was blunt about what they did and confronted them with the issue, *"You meant evil against me, but God meant it for good..."* (Genesis 50:20 NKJV).

King Solomon tells us that overlooking a transgression is to a person's glory. The word *overlook* means to set aside or go beyond. The Hebrew word for *forgiveness* means to release. True forgiveness means that we must make a choice not to hold the offense against them in the future. Forgiveness isn't a feeling or a word—it's a choice. Solomon is emphatic when he says that when you chose to forgive, you will receive glory!

3. Great leaders invest in themselves.

In an article in the CNBC online edition, billionaire Warren Buffett was quoted as saying there is one investment that supersedes all others: "Ultimately, there's one investment that supersedes all others: Invest in yourself. Nobody can take away what you've got in yourself, and everybody has potential they haven't used yet."[13]

There it is, that word *potential*" Buffett used it, and I could not agree more that all of us have untapped potential. A common definition of the word *potential* is latent qualities or abilities that may be developed and lead to future success or usefulness.

In the world of sports, millions will be paid to some college kid who has never put on an NBA uniform based on his potential. He may have been great in college, but they are not paying him a huge signing bonus for the last year of his college career, they are paying for what he might do in the future. As a side note, I've written an entire book about potential titled *How to Release Your Full Potential* that you may want to read.

Add value to your existing stock. In the real world, we don't get paid based on potential. It just doesn't work that way. I heard one leadership expert say, "The more you learn, the more you earn!" I say, "If it stays in your head, you're dead. But if it gets in your heart, you're smart!" There is a correlation between how much you know and how much value you bring to the table. If your car breaks down on the highway, who would add more value to your situation? A plumber or a mechanic? I'm guessing you would want the one who has trained and worked in the area of your need. The mechanic is the logical and only choice, unless your car has a commode in it that's not working!

Charles "Tremendous" Jones said, "You will be the same in five years as you are today except for the people you meet and the books you read."[14] A significant factor that separates the "talkers" from the "doers" is a concerted effort to grow and invest in your success. How do you do that? By becoming a lifelong investor—not in stocks and bonds or real estate, but in yourself!

Take a ride on the information highway. Think about the fact that in today's world, we have instant access to more information than any other period in human history. Even the smart phone you have in your hand can gain access to the information that only a few decades ago would have been unthinkable.

The bottom line—there is no excuse for not investing in your growth. Start today and pick up a book, listen to a CD, or attend a seminar. The most successful companies in the world spend billions of dollars on research and development, so maybe that's why they are so successful. Make up your mind to resign from the "Someday" club. You know the motto, "Someday I'm going to start...." And join the "I'm doing it now" club!

A Final Thought

Remember, when the door of opportunity opens, it will be too late to prepare! Joel Osteen declared, "I want to challenge you today to get out of your comfort zone. You have so much incredible potential on the inside. God has put gifts and talents in you that you probably don't know anything about."[15]

When is a good time to start preparing for your success? How about today?

> *Here is what I have seen: It is good and fitting for one to eat and drink, and to **enjoy the good of all his labor** in which he toils under the sun all the days of his life which God gives him; for it is his heritage. As for every man to whom God has given riches and wealth, and given him*

*power to eat of it, to receive his heritage and rejoice in his labor—this is **the gift of God**. For he will not dwell unduly on the days of his life, because **God keeps him busy with the joy of his heart** (Ecclesiastes 5:18-20 NKJV).*

6

GREAT LEADERS REMAIN COACHABLE IN SPITE OF THEIR SUCCESS

Whoever loves discipline loves knowledge, but whoever hates correction is stupid.

—PROVERBS 12:1

Just like golf, leadership is a game that provides a lifetime opportunity for improvement. To improve in golf requires a focus and a willingness to make mistakes in order to progress. Leadership also requires a willingness to make mistakes and to focus on one shot at a time. This way you make every action count.

—ESTHER EWING[1]

Introduction

The game of golf has been in my blood since I started golfing in my forties. I have had the privilege of playing some of the most

83

beautiful golf courses in this country as well as Canada and Mexico. However, it only took a few years of playing the game to learn two valuable lessons:

- *First,* I discovered golf is a fickle game. One day you're in love with the game, and everything feels right. You hit the links, and the grass is extra green, the sky is bright and beautiful, and even the birds are singing your praises on every shot. But, you go out the next day and try to repeat everything you did the day before, and it's as if you never played the game. And, before the round is over, you are ready to throw your clubs in the nearest body of water.

- *Second,* I learned that golf is a game that can only be played, but never perfected by mere mortals. Golf is no respecter of persons, period. I don't care if your name is Woods, Nicklaus, or Palmer, the minute you think you have it figured out, she will reach up and grab you by the throat and let you know that she cannot be conquered! Once I came to grips with those two things, my enjoyment level went up, and my frustration level went down.

Numerous lessons can be learned about life in general and leadership in particular from the game of golf. It doesn't matter whether you are an avid participant, a casual observer, or never played the game, there are still principles all can learn.

Daniel Newman, CEO of Broadsuite Media Group, observed:

Golf is a hobby to many. They play the game passionately and with high expectations even though for many it is played only sporadically. These high expectations combined with passion can also yield immense frustration as golf is an incredibly difficult game for even the most avid player. However, it often takes only a single great shot to makes all the pain and adversity entirely worthwhile. Ultimately it is what will keep you coming back to the links for years to come.

Leadership can be the same way. Those who are most active at it are often doing it out of passion and a desire to improve (self or others). This desire to change, inspire, and impassion can deliver amazing results one day only to bring dismal results the next. Nevertheless, when leadership and passion are a part of your DNA, quitting is never an option. So, the choice becomes to persevere and to be a lifelong learner.[2]

Five of My Favorite Golf Leadership Lessons

1. *Start with the fundamentals.*

A *fundamental* as defined by Merriam-Webster.com is "serving as a basis supporting existence or determining essential structure or function: of central importance." A fundamental is a core principle that is basic to any endeavor, whether sports, business, or education. Without the fundamentals serving as a foundation, whatever is being built will eventually fall from its weight.

- *In golf or any sport for that matter, the key is learning the fundamentals.* A good and wise golf instructor will stress the importance of the basics, such as: proper grip, maintaining balance, and keeping your eye on the ball. While some beginners want to make sure they have the same equipment the pros use, a sound teacher will stress the fundamentals over how you "look" on the first tee.

- *How do fundamentals apply to leadership?* Becoming a leader is not about a title—it's about function. I have known some who thought that having a title was the end of itself. There are others who successfully function as leaders without a title.

There are dozens of books and articles that list the "fundamentals of leadership." Some lists are short and some are long, but they all agree on one thing—unless you are willing to learn and practice the basics, success is only a pipe dream.

My list of fundamentals includes the following, but is not limited to:

1. Communicate the core values of the organization.
2. Build trust in the team, and it starts at the top.
3. Learn to manage your time, or it will manage you.
4. Share the vision of the organization.
5. Lead with integrity.

Consultant Jeffrey Carter shares the following on the importance of learning the fundamentals:

Basic fundamentals are important in any business. They are also important for success in athletics. Sometimes, there is only one way to do something. In order to perfect it, you drill on that specific skill over and over again. It's boring, but in the heat of the moment when you need to rely on it—that skill just happens. You don't even have to think about it.[3]

2. Practice doesn't always make perfect.

I am sure you have heard the old saying, "Practice makes perfect." That may be true in other areas of life, but I have never met anyone who practiced enough to become "perfect" when it comes to the game of golf! I believe that practicing the fundamentals of the game is necessary, not to become perfect, but to simply get better.

Practice doesn't make perfect, especially if you practice the wrong thing. Practice doesn't make perfect, but it does make permanent. The object of practicing the fundamentals of the game is to build muscle memory. Therefore, you can stay on the practice range until your hands bleed, but if you are creating muscle memory without honing proper fundamentals, all you are doing is perfecting a bad swing!

I must admit, because of my schedule, there have been times when I had to choose between practicing or playing. Most of the time, I chose the latter instead of the former. That does not mean that I do not value the time spent on the practice range. I am convinced that one quality hour spent practicing the proper fundamentals is better than six hours practicing it the wrong way.

How does practice apply to leadership? Golf professional Sean Foley observed:

> If you've ever wondered why you can't replicate that swing you grooved on the range when you play golf, it's because traditional practice habits have about as much to do with performing on the golf course as running on a treadmill does to competing in the Boston Marathon. Sure, to play

better golf, practicing your swing mechanics is important. But at some point, if you're not preparing yourself for what a round of golf is really all about, your time on the practice tee will be little more than just that—time on the practice tee.[4]

As I've said, golf is about improvement, not perfection. The same attitude can be found in a wise leader who knows that trying to become perfect is a losing proposition. But, to create a winning atmosphere, the leader must be willing to work on areas of improvement that will benefit the entire team.

Four areas that might need improvement:

- *Vision.* Have I made the vision clear enough so that the least member of my organization and or staff could answer what we are all about and where we are going?
- *Atmosphere.* Have I created an environment that is conducive to improving the entire organization, not just those at the top of the food chain?
- *Mistakes.* Have I been open and honest with my team when things don't go as planned?
- *Communication.* Most importantly, am I communicating with my mentor on a consistent basis?

3. *A Bad Start Doesn't Equal a Bad Finish*

PGA professional Peter Jacobsen remarked, "One of the most fascinating things about golf is how it reflects the cycle of life. No matter what you shoot, the next day you have to go back to the first tee and begin all over again and make yourself into something."[5]

There are many adjectives used to describe the game of golf. Most I cannot repeat here, but suffice it to say the game can make even the strongest people beg for mercy. But there is a two-word phrase I've used many times to describe the game, "Second chances." You can make a horrible score on the first hole, and yet when you get to the next hole, you have been given a second chance to make a better score. Golf is a game that says, "You still have time to make something good out of a bad start!"

- *If things don't start well, it may be time for "course" corrections.* The object of golf is to make more good shots than bad ones. Even the greatest players of the game understand that in every round of golf there will be misses, mistakes, and miscalculations. The great Ben Hogan said, "This is a game of misses. The guy who misses the best is going to win."[6]

- *How do "course corrections" apply to leadership?* Obviously, keeping bad shots to a minimum is the goal. But, once a lousy shot happens, and it will, you don't dwell on it. You move on to the next shot and hopefully do better. The same is true in leadership. Things are going to go wrong; you can count on it. It is never "if"; it's always "when."

Here are three ways to make a course correction:

- *Be willing to make necessary changes.* Making essential changes that lead to improvement is vital, whether it is hitting a golf ball or developing a winning organization. If what we have been doing is not working, don't be afraid to go in a different direction. Each of us can transform every area of our life—it's called the power of choice.

- *Accept responsibility for what went wrong.* I don't know how many times I have hit a bad shot during a round of golf and wanted desperately to blame the club! I've watched some of the greatest golfers in the world hit bad shots and turn and scream at their caddy. Yelling at the club or the caddy will not fix the problem. If there is any blame, it falls on the shoulders of the one who hit it! If something goes wrong, it is up to the leadership to deal with the issues, which is called taking responsibility.

- *Know when to go for it and when to lay up.* One of the best ways to stay out of trouble on the golf course is to try to hit the ball in the fairway—aka the *short grass.* If I am always afraid of hitting the ball in the hazards, I can be sure my score is not going to be good. There are times in life when going for it is the smart move, and there are other times when it's wise to slow down and consider the fallout of a bad decision.

4. *Even Champions Need a Coach*

It is not just a fashion statement when a world-class athlete like Tiger Woods shows up on the practice tee with a coach by his side. The trend for swing coaches has been on the upswing for several decades now, with most if not all golfers relying on another set of eyes to help fix any problems that may arise. I have seen amateurs, professionals, and even those we might consider world champions make use of a coach.

Why is that? World-famous sports psychologist Bob Rotella, in an interview with *Golf Digest,* said the following about the need for coaching:

> I don't think any golfer is totally self-reliant. Most of them work with a teacher. There's no denying that a big piece of this game is that you have to learn the skills, and coaches help with that. But then you have to learn to go out on the golf course and trust it and play golf, and the week of the tournament, that's done alone.
>
> On the other hand, depth of competition is driving more coaching. Just like in football the coaching staffs are getting bigger and bigger; golf has more coaches. The more money players make, the more they can hire specialists to help them in specific areas. The truth is, there aren't many people who can figure it out on their own. So, golfers have to find that happy balance.[7]

Are you coachable? As mentioned previously, one of the best days of my life happened when I learned to say a simple three-word phrase, "I don't know." Those three little words changed my life forever. That statement is my confession that I don't know everything; and the good news is, I don't have to know everything to be successful! When I don't have all the answers to whatever challenges I might be facing, I seek out someone who does know how to help me navigate through the trouble.

In August 2013, The Miles Group and Stanford University conducted an Executive Coaching Survey that revealed: "'Lonely at the top' resonates for most CEOs. Nearly two-thirds of CEOs do not receive coaching or leadership advice from outside consultants or coaches, and almost half of senior executives are not receiving any either."[8]

A majority of CEOs agree that coaching is essential, but the survey revealed that 66 percent of those senior executives do not receive coaching or leadership advice from outside sources. The conclusion is obvious. It is one thing to say you believe that coaching is essential, but saying it is not equivalent to receiving it!

The most common excuse I have heard as to why some leaders don't use a coach is lack of resources. That's like saying I can't lose weight or exercise regularly because I don't have the money to hire a personal trainer at the gym. If you want something bad enough, you will find a way to make it happen.

Money is really not the issue because there are plenty of books, conferences, and online resources available to anyone willing to utilize them. The organization I pastor has one of the greatest personal mentorship/coaching programs available. But, you must avail yourself to what's available.

Learn the difference between a consultant and a coach. Consultants are usually "hired guns" brought in to point out where things have gone wrong. They are like the proverbial gunslingers who stepped out in the street to "draw down" on all potential threats to the organization. I'm not saying that's all bad all the time, but there may be a better way to do things.

A coach is someone who may point out where things have gone off the rails and is willing to stay with you until the trouble areas are fixed. Consultants are good, and sometimes necessary, but coaches are better.

Author and leadership coach Lolly Daskal says:

Good leaders are passionate and committed, authentic, courageous, honest and reliable. But in today's high-pressure environment, leaders need a confidante, a coach—someone they can trust to tell the truth about their struggles, which is a difficult role for others within the same organization to fill. That's where coaches truly earn their keep.[9]

5. *Play by the Rules*

The adage "Rules are made to be broken" does not apply to the game of golf. Someone famously said that golf is the only sport where the person playing the game can call a penalty on themselves. Golf is made up of rules and traditions dating back hundreds of years; and even though we may not always agree, rules are there for a purpose. Rules rightly applied are like the banks of a river. The banks are not there for punishment, but to keep the powerful currents flowing in the right direction.

> Adhering to the Rules of Golf connects us to golfers all over the world, and adds a sense of pride to our accomplishments on the course.
>
> —STEVEN GIBBONS, *USGA*[10]

A wise leader will play by the rules. Can you be successful without playing by the rules? I suppose anything is possible if you try hard enough. But why would anyone want to get ahead in life or business by breaking the rules?

My Top Three Rules for Success

1. The Team Rule

Everyone has a choice to strike out on their own or be part of a team. Many people decide to travel the leadership highway alone. Somehow they think by *not* carrying passengers along for the ride is better because it gives them a sense of freedom. As a result, whatever obstacles, detours, or breakdowns might occur, they have no one to call on for help. Traveling alone is not always the best way to go.

Whether in sports or business, the greatest accomplishments can be attributed to the work of teams focused on a common goal to achieve unified results.

Instead of being a loner, consider what a team can do:

- A team can make you better than you ever dreamed possible.
- Your value will be multiplied exponentially.
- Teamwork allows you the opportunity to focus on your best.
- Becoming a team member helps you help others.
- It will provide you an arena to see the desires of your heart fulfilled.

Good leaders make people feel that they're at the very heart of things, not at the periphery. Everyone feels that he or she makes a difference to the success of the organization. When that happens, people feel centered and that gives their work meaning.[11]

2. *The Trust Rule*

Trying to build any business organization without trust is like trying to lay brick without the cement. It might look sturdy, but it will not last, especially when foul weather hits. Trust allows each person to have confidence that all the intentions of team members are good and for the benefit of everyone. Surprisingly, when trust is built among the team, the fear of asking questions is removed.

Lack of trust is easy to spot if you know what you are looking for:

- The success of the individual becomes more important than the entire team.
- Communication will break down.
- The group becomes polarized and politicized.
- Team members will be afraid to share criticism.

  When you know that someone needs you, cares about you, appreciates you, respects you, believes in you, and accepts you with all your imperfections, trust and harmony are nurtured.[12]

Building trust is like making deposits in a bank. But each time trust is broken, we are making withdrawals. Any banker will tell you when you try to make withdrawals without sufficient funds, you have a major problem.

How do we make trust deposits?

- *Share.* It's almost impossible to trust someone you don't know. Knowing one another is the first step to building trust.

- *Talk.* Discuss former team experiences such as what worked well and what didn't. This will go a long way in building trust with the current team.

- *Have courage.* Dare to share your strengths and weaknesses honestly with teammates. Everybody has some. You might be surprised at their reaction, so go for it!

- *Listen.* As I have said before, God has given us two ears and one mouth. Is it possible He wants us to listen twice as much as we talk? One surefire way to kill team spirit is always having to say something about everything, and acting like an expert when you're not. The unpardonable sin of a team member is to have absolutely nothing to say, and go ahead and say it anyway!

3. *The Test Rule*

When I say "test," I am not talking about school, but a test of our commitment to the overall goals. In golf or any sport, it's called being "sold out"—not holding anything back. An "all-in" kind of commitment is at the core of success. And you can count on one thing, your commitment will be tested. Being committed to doing the things that others won't, or don't, separates you from the pack.

> To achieve your potential or live your real possibilities, somewhere deep in your core you have to choose to go after your dreams. You also have to create an underlying belief that you can do it. When you dream big dreams, and focus on the little daily steps that will take you there, you nourish your long-term commitment, your focus, your confidence, and your belief in your mission.[13]

A Final Thought

Malcolm Gladwell wrote in his book *Outliers: The Story of Success:*

> To become a chess grandmaster also seems to take about
> ten years. (Only the legendary Bobby Fischer got to that
> elite level in less than that amount of time: it took him
> nine years.) And what's ten years? Well, it's roughly how
> long it takes to put in ten thousand hours of hard practice.
> Ten thousand hours is the magic number of greatness.[14]

Commitment to action is an essential characteristic of a capable
team. Remember, just by talking about something does not ensure
success. Any champion will tell you it takes more than just dreaming
about success to win. Most of the time we see only the finished product; whether it is an Olympic gold medal or a PGA Championship.

What we don't see is what goes on when the average but motivated and committed person is at the gym, in the pool, at the
keyboard, or on the putting green for hours on end. To become an
"overnight success" requires many months, even years before the hard
work pays off.

7

GREAT LEADERS POSSESS THE "X FACTOR"

Not so with you. Instead, whoever wants to become great among you must be your servant, and whoever wants to be first must be your slave— just as the Son of Man did not come to be served, but to serve, and to give his life as a ransom for many.

—MATTHEW 20:26-28

Servant leadership is a blend and balance between leader and servant. You don't lose leadership qualities when becoming a servant leader.

—SKIP PRICHARD[1]

Introduction

Several years ago, a music competition was launched in the United Kingdom called *The X Factor*. The show was the brainchild of a man everyone loves to hate, British producer Simon Cowell. *The X Factor* as defined by one of its judges is that "something you can't quite put your finger on."[2] The X factor has also been defined as the "undefinable," something that makes a star, or possess star quality. It's one of those qualities that may not appear on the surface. But as soon as you are in the presence of such individuals, you know there is something different about them.

When it comes to qualities of leadership, I like to think of the X factor as the missing ingredient that many leaders want, but few are willing to pay the price to have. In working with leaders from every conceivable background, skill level, and educational achievement, I have discovered that the ones who rise above the rest are the ones who possess the number-one key ingredient that makes them successful—the X factor.

What is the X factor that many leaders lack? Can this trait be developed, or is it something that either you have it, or you don't? Before I share with you my insight on the matter, let's see what others suggest the X factor could be.

From casual observation, it appears everyone has an opinion. The following are three of the most popular ideas regarding the question, "What is the X factor?"

What Is the X Factor?

1. *Organizational Culture*

Akintola Benson-Oke writing for *Vanguard* online quoted Mike Myatt of *Forbes* magazine who says that *organizational culture* is the missing *X factor*.

> There are those who argue that leaders are born such that, once a person is not born to be a leader, he or she becomes forever incapable of occupying leadership

positions. This is what is popularly referred to as the 'X Factor'. Mike Myatt, writing for Forbes Magazine, opined that the 'X Factor' is one's culture, one's total approach to doing things. He said, it is the "Great Culture...that every organisation strives to attain but few achieve. It's often talked about, but rarely understood. Culture is in fact more than a buzzword—it's the very lifeblood of an organization. Culture is what develops and sustains an enterprise. Every organization has a culture. The question CEOs must ask of themselves is do they have the culture they need? Culture must be more than an afterthought— it must be intentional, purposed, and created by design; not by default."[3]

2. Executive Presence

Suzanne Bates, CEO and founder of Bates coaching and consulting firm, conducted extensive research and concluded that the X factor is "executive presence." She writes that the executive presence, "can be defined in three dimensions: character, substance, and style." She goes on to say, "We now know that these are the qualities of leadership that enable executives to inspire commitment, mobilize above-and-beyond effort, and elevate organizational performance."[4]

3. Integrity

When it comes to leadership, there can be no doubt about the importance of integrity. I find that integrity is so valuable that later in this book I devote an entire chapter on the subject. The word *integrity* as defined by Merriam-Webster is "firm adherence to a code of especially moral or artistic values: the quality or state of being complete or undivided." Integrity is the bedrock of character that we must demonstrate if we are ever going to have successful, meaningful lives.

Thomas Jefferson said, "I am sure that in estimating every man's value either in private or public life, a pure integrity is the quality we take first into calculation, and that learning and talents are only the second."[5]

While I agree that creating the right *organizational culture*, providing an *executive presence*, along with *integrity* are key elements in leadership success, I hasten to add that there is one trait often overlooked, misapplied, and misunderstood. I contend there is one key intangible trait that must become the foundation for everything we are trying to accomplish.

What is the X factor I am referring too? Servant leadership.

There are three identifiable characteristics of a servant leader: humility; sink or swim attitude, open to accountability. Let's define each in more depth.

Characteristic 1—Humility

The dictionary's definition of *humility* is "freedom from pride or arrogance: the quality or state of being humble." It is unfortunate that when discussing humility, the word is often confused with weakness, or in today's language, being a doormat. Just mention the word *humility*, and you will hear individual attitudes such as:

- Humility means I'm gullible and will fall for any scam that comes along.
- If I show any hint of humility at my work, I'll get run over.
- I don't need to be humble; I'll leave that to others.

- Humility means I don't have it all together, and that's not me!

Mick Ukleja observes:

> We live in a world that favors the strong. In that context, "meekness" is often confused with "weakness." Nothing could be further from the truth. Meekness is a power word. In the ancient world, it was often used to describe the winning horse in a race; they were called meek, which meant "strength under control." The horse was tamed, but not timid. This is also true for our perception of humility. To make the distinction, let's call it healthy humility. Contrary to popular belief, humility is not "thinking less of yourself"—it's "thinking of yourself less."[6]

The other side of the humility coin is pride. The theme song for many people I have encountered could be from an old song by singer/songwriter Mac Davis. The critical line says, "Oh Lord it's hard to be humble, when you're perfect in every way. I can't wait to look in the mirror, cause I get better lookin' each day."[7]

Rob McKinnon says that pride is the opposite of humility: "The reality is that we are all arrogant at times—and pride underlies most of our vices. This is why humility is key. It is the effective antidote, enabling most of the other virtues of good character."[8]

A study on the subject of humility, as it relates to leadership concluded:

> Humility may be a virtue. It's also a competitive advantage. According to a study from the University of Washington Foster School of Business, humble people

are more likely to be high performers in individual and team settings. They also tend to make the most effective leaders. "Humility is an important component of effective leadership in modern organizations," says co-author Michael Johnson, an associate professor of management at the Foster School. "Humble leaders foster learning-oriented teams and engage employees. They also optimize job satisfaction and employee retention."[9]

It is hard to identify something if you don't know what it is. Trying to put labels on someone can be tricky at best, and fraught with danger at worst. Why? Unless you have the X-ray vision of Superman, it's impossible to look into people's hearts to know if they are real or fake. The best way to identify "humble" leaders is to listen to their words, observe their attitudes, and watch their actions. In my experience, if people keep telling you how humble they are, they probably aren't. It's usually the ones who don't know they are...who are! You don't have to advertise humility—it will speak for itself.

Craig Impelman, in an article for *Success.com*, wrote about the necessary qualities of a humble leader and pointed out an example from the world of college basketball. He refers to Coach John Wooden who led the UCLA basketball team to some of the greatest feats ever seen in college basketball. But it was not just the victories that made Coach Wooden so successful. It was his attitude of humility and a willingness to serve others that made the difference in the lives of so many players, coaches, and fans.

Impelman shares:

In Pat Williams's book *How to Be Like Coach Wooden*, there is an entire chapter titled "If You Want to Be Like

Coach, Strive for Humility." In that chapter, Coach Wooden's grandson Greg described Coach:

My grandfather is an extremely humble man. He's led by example his whole life and stayed true to his beliefs. He's never asked anyone to do anything he wouldn't do himself.

Coach Wooden's teams always left their locker room, home or away, cleaner than the way they found it. ...Franklin Adler, a student manager for the UCLA basketball team from 1964 to 1968, recalls an incident when he was cleaning up after a game that reflects Coach's humility:

I was scurrying around between banks of lockers when I heard the sound of footsteps and the thud of objects landing in a receptacle. Thankful for any help, I assumed that a Washington State janitorial employee was making his rounds after the game. Imagine my surprise when I came around a corner and saw that my ally in cleaning up the room was Coach Wooden![10]

Characteristic 2—Sink or Swim: We Are ALL in the Same Boat

Sad to say many people decide the "Lone Ranger" approach is better than joining a team. Why? It gives them a sense of independence. If you want to accomplish your dreams, it's going to take more than individual talent to get there. Wise leaders will do everything possible to serve something greater than themselves. The best place to start is to foster a "we are all in the same boat together" attitude among those with whom you lead.

Be thankful for the role that you are in and that you have been placed in a position to lead others—it is an honor. Share your gratitude to the people you lead for the work and sacrifices they make.

—THUY SINDELL, *PhD and Milo Sindell, MS*[11]

Three Ways You Can Serve Others:

1.   Be more interested in helping others succeed is a good start. You may be familiar with the saying, "What you make happen for others, the Lord will make happen for you." That statement may sound like a well-worn cliché, but I happen to believe it's true. I've seen the results of investing time, energy, and resources into helping others achieve their dreams. And in turn, I have watched how the Lord has moved mountains to bring an abundant harvest into my family, business, and relationships.

I have lived by the Luke 6:38 principle for many years. If you don't know it, learn it, and live it, and watch what God will do in your life. Jesus said, *"Give, and it will be given to you. A good measure, pressed down, shaken together, and running over, will be poured into your lap. For with the measure you use, it will be measured to you."* Remember this: whenever you release what is in your hand, God will release what is in His hand. And trust me, what He has for you is far greater than anything you can do for yourself!

2.   Remember where you came from. Why is it important that servant leaders remember where they came from? One of the hidden dangers of success is developing a faulty memory, which produces an attitude of "ingratitude." No matter how high you climb, servant leaders will look behind to see how they can help boost those who maybe are on the lowest rung of the ladder of success. Nothing kills the positive atmosphere of an organization like leaders who think they are "too good" to get down in the trenches and slug it out like the rest of the folks.

> Always do everything you ask of those you command.
> —GENERAL GEORGE S. PATTON[12]

3.   *Give freely.* You may be where you are today because someone gave of their time and resources to help you. I doubt there was ever any expectation of a return on that investment in your life.

Now it is time for you to pay it forward and invest in someone who needs your input. Whether it is in ministry or business, the most significant accomplishments can be attributed to the work of teams focused on a common goal to achieve unified results.

> A servant-leader focuses primarily on the growth and well-being of people and the communities to which they belong. While traditional leadership generally involves the accumulation and exercise of power by one at the "top of the pyramid," servant leadership is different. The servant-leader shares power, puts the needs of others first and helps people develop and perform as highly as possible.[13]

Characteristic 3—Open to Accountability

A true servant-leader does not shy away from accountability. A part of accountability is a willingness to admit and correct mistakes. Lack of accountability produces confusion, distrust, and lack of respect. Michael Hyatt writes about how leaders demonstrate accountability: "Everyone wants to be a leader. However, few are prepared to accept the accountability that goes with it. But you can't have one without the other. They are two sides of the same coin."[14]

The dictionary definition of *accountability* includes taking responsibility for the outcome, whether it is good or bad: "the quality or state of being accountable: especially: an obligation or willingness *to accept responsibility* or to account for one's actions."

Why is it so necessary to accept responsibility for our actions? Simple. If we don't, who will? Sadly, we have watched the growth of a generation of "Monday morning quarterbacks." The term refers to those who watch the game on Sunday and then spend Monday pointing out all the mistakes made by their favorite team. It is so much easier to criticize others than to play the game yourself.

I used to hear that baseball was our national pastime. Not anymore. Avoiding responsibility is now our new national pastime, and it's getting worse. For instance:

- If you have cancer from smoking cigarettes, blame the tobacco industry, but whatever you do don't take responsibility for lighting up your first smoke!

- If you drive under the influence of alcohol, blame the bar for selling you the drinks, but don't take responsibility for crashing your car and killing innocent people.

- If the IRS garnishes your pay because you failed to pay your taxes, blame H&R Block for their failure to come to your home and file your taxes for you.

- If your doctor tells you that you must lose weight or you are going experience major health problems, then by all means blame the food industry for making you eat too much pizza and ice cream. But, don't take responsibility for losing weight and getting into better shape.

If I spend all my time justifying my mistakes by pointing the finger at someone or something else, all I'm doing is avoiding responsibility. The bottom line—if I want things to change, I have to do it myself. All the finger pointing in the world won't change one single thing in my life!

When it comes to avoiding personal responsibility, look no farther than many, if not most, of today's colleges and universities. What a difference a few generations make. In June 1944, eighteen and nineteen-year-olds were storming the beaches of Normandy, while many of today's eighteen and nineteen-year-olds are looking for "safe spaces," and eliminating "trigger words." The differences between the "I-give generation" and the "Give-me generation."

Dr. Everett Piper, former Oklahoma Wesleyan University president, addressed a situation that occurred when one his students became upset when the speaker at chapel talked about love from First Corinthians 13. The student said the message made him feel "bad for not showing love," and "the speaker was wrong for making him and his peers feel uncomfortable."

Dr. Piper spoke directly to the situation in an open letter to all students, faulty, and board members. The transcript follows:

> Dr. Everett Piper, President
>
> Oklahoma Wesleyan University
>
> This past week, I actually had a student come forward after a university chapel service and complain because he felt "victimized" by a sermon on the topic of 1 Corinthians 13. It appears this young scholar felt offended because a homily on love made him feel bad for not showing love. In his mind, the speaker was wrong for making him, and his peers, feel uncomfortable.

I'm not making this up. Our culture has actually taught our kids to be this self-absorbed and narcissistic. Any time their feelings are hurt, they are the victims. Anyone who dares challenge them and, thus, makes them "feel bad" about themselves, is a "hater," a "bigot," an "oppressor," and a "victimizer."

I have a message for this young man and all others who care to listen. That feeling of discomfort you have after listening to a sermon is called a conscience. An altar call is supposed to make you feel bad. It is supposed to make you feel guilty. The goal of many a good sermon is to get you to confess your sins—not coddle you in your selfishness. The primary objective of the Church and the Christian faith is your confession, not your self-actualization.

So here's my advice:

If you want the chaplain to tell you you're a victim rather than tell you that you need virtue, this may not be the university you're looking for. If you want to complain about a sermon that makes you feel less than loving for not showing love, this might be the wrong place.

If you're more interested in playing the "hater" card than you are in confessing your own hate; if you want to arrogantly lecture, rather than humbly learn; if you don't want to feel guilt in your soul when you are guilty of sin; if you want to be enabled rather than confronted, there are many universities across the land (in Missouri and elsewhere) that will give you exactly what you want, but Oklahoma Wesleyan isn't one of them.

At OKWU, we teach you to be selfless rather than self-centered. We are more interested in you practicing personal forgiveness than political revenge. We want you to model interpersonal reconciliation rather than foment personal conflict. We believe the content of your character is more important than the color of your skin. We don't believe that you have been victimized every time you feel guilty and we don't issue "trigger warnings" before altar calls.

Oklahoma Wesleyan is not a "safe place," but rather, a place to learn: to learn that life isn't about you, but about others; that the bad feeling you have while listening to a sermon is called guilt; that the way to address it is to repent of everything that's wrong with you rather than blame others for everything that's wrong with them. This is a place where you will quickly learn that you need to grow up.

This is not a day care. This is a university.[15]

Author's note: I am shouting AMEN to this letter at the top of my voice! If we had more leaders like Dr. Piper, maybe more of this generation would learn what being accountable and taking responsibility is all about.

Some in this generation of leaders may need a new introduction to President Harry Truman's philosophy of leadership accountability. On President Truman's desk was the sign that read: THE BUCK STOPS HERE! The desk plaque was more than a cute ornament; it was a nonverbal statement reflecting that he was accountable and responsible for his actions. How refreshing would it be for this and every generation to incorporate his leadership style.

"The Buck Stops Here" means: 1) refusing to blame others for our mistakes; and 2) refusing to take the path of least resistance.

1)Refusing to blame others for our mistakes. The blame game has been perfected in the 21st century. What started in an ideal environment made for success, has now degenerated into "Who can I blame for my failures, mistakes, and general screwups?"

> No one is a failure until they blame somebody else.
> —CHARLES "TREMENDOUS" JONES[16]

- Husbands blame their wives because they nag too much.
- Wives blame their husbands for not being more emotionally involved in their needs.
- Teenagers blame their parents for being too strict and not understanding their feelings.
- The "down-line" blames the "up-line" for not giving them enough tools for success, and compassionate understanding.
- The "up-line" blames the "down-line" for not working harder, even if that could cause their failure.

On and on it goes because there's always someone else you can find to blame for your failures.

> The man who can smile when things go wrong has thought of someone else he can blame it on.
> —ROBERT BLOCH, *Of Wit and Humor*

One of the first lessons you learn in the military is if you have a problem never take it to someone of lower rank. Why? The person of lower rank will hear your problems, but has no authority to do anything to change or fix it. You always take your problems to someone above you. A sergeant does not take issues to a private. He or she goes to the one above, usually the company commander. Problems are compounded when we discuss our issues with those who can't fix them—and that's called gossip and or sour grapes.

The same principles apply in business. If you're facing challenges and difficulties, never take your problems to someone who can't solve them or has no power or authority to change it. Always think "up" not "down." And know that the blame game always comes full circle, back to the one who started it. There is hope, though, the blame game can be overcome, especially when we realize its many pitfalls and booby traps.

2)Refusing to take the path of least resistance. A servant leader knows there may be situations where the best way to get things done is to take responsibility and do it yourself!

> Without accountability, even the most brilliant, hard-working, well-intentioned leaders fail—they fail to meet their performance goals, they fail to develop their teams, they fail to hire top talent, they fail to coach their employees, they fail to communicate clearly, they fail to optimize performance, and they fail the business overall. Effective leadership requires real accountability.[17]

A Final Thought

It is vitally important to establish a culture of servant leadership. It is past time for those of us who have enjoyed the freedom to live out our dreams to make sure we don't forget those who need our help.

How do we do that?

First, we can *lead by example.* It is not enough to simply tell others about the importance of serving one another. We must be willing to show by our actions, not just our words.

Second, to establish this kind of culture, we must be willing to make an effort to invest in the lives of those who are above us—as well as those below us in our organization.

Just by doing those two things, we can change the atmosphere all the way from the mailroom to the board room. Servant leadership, in my opinion, is the missing *X factor* in most leadership.

Great Leaders Live Productive Intentional Lives

*Friends, don't get me wrong: By no means do I count
myself an expert in all of this, but I've got my eye on the
goal, where God is beckoning us onward—to Jesus. I'm off
and running, and I'm not turning back.*
—Philippians 3:13-14 MSG

Be fearless in the pursuit of what sets your soul on fire.
—Author Unknown

Introduction

On July 20, 1969, Neil Armstrong became the first man to step on
the moon, and uttered the most famous statement in human history:
"That's one small step for a man, one giant leap for mankind."

Armstrong's words echoed the actual event, but the intention to
land on the moon started almost a decade earlier. On May 25, 1961,
President John Kennedy stood before a joint session of Congress
and declared:

I believe that this nation should commit itself to achieving the goal, before this decade is out, of landing a man on the moon and returning him safely to the Earth. No single space project in this period will be more impressive to mankind, or more important for the long-range exploration of space; and none will be so difficult or expensive to accomplish.[1]

President Kennedy's "intention" was to challenge Congress, and the nation, to set aside the necessary funds to take the bold steps to land a man on the moon and bring him back safely to the earth. If over the next eight years nothing happened to bring us closer to his stated goals, then his speech would have been nothing more than the musing of a visionary with no action plan to achieve the desired results. But immediately after his speech, the wheels began to turn, and on July 20, 1969, the entire world saw the results.

According to the Routledge Encyclopedia of Philosophy, "intentionality" is "the mind's capacity to direct itself on things. Mental states like thoughts, beliefs, desires, hopes (and others) exhibit intentionality in the sense that they are always directed on, or at, something." Therefore, when our actions back up our intentions, we cannot only "intend" to shoot for the moon, but we can be assured of success.

You can go to any period of history and find certain leaders we remember and study who were intentional about what they wanted to accomplish.

Examples include:

- American Revolutionary War hero, John Paul Jones. Things didn't happen to him; he made them happen. He said, "I wish to have no connection with any ship that does not sail fast; for I *intend* to go in harm's way."

- Witness Winston Churchill, who certainly did not start World War II, but he approached it on his front foot saying, "History will be kind to me for I *intend* to write it."

- Then there are those who lead in circumstances they did not choose. John F. Kennedy used to downplay his role in saving the crew of PT 109 in World War II, saying, "It was involuntary. They sank my boat." But, like John Paul Jones, Kennedy chose to go into harm's way—he chose to tow his crew members to safety. That is intentional leadership.[2]

Dr. Randy Carlson, in his book *The Power of One Thing,* explains the secret to living an intentional life:

> It's as simple as the following formula: Information + Insight + Action = Intentional Living.
>
> *Information* represents the facts you need to know about your situation—you need to know the total of all your debts, how high your blood pressure is, or what grades your struggling child is getting school.
>
> *Insight* is being able to look at a problem in an analytical thoughtful way, asking God to give you wisdom and discernment so you know what to do or what course to follow.
>
> *Action* means you start doing something about the information and insights you have gathered. Without action,

nothing happens. These three components make up intentional living.[3]

Carlson is right. Having information about what we want to accomplish is necessary, but it is not enough. Information without following up with insight and action leads to a life of frustration and limited productivity. For instance, if I know I am overweight and I intend to do something about it, I can step on my scale and get all the information I need. The scale may tell me I am thirty pounds overweight, but what it cannot do is devise a plan of action that will help me reach my goal.

The bottom line is this: *Good intentions don't always translate into productivity.* I know many people who start every new year vowing to get in shape, add more income, or whatever else they failed to accomplish in the past year. Sadly, of the 43 percent who start the new year with good intentions, only about 8 percent will achieve any measure of success.

Thomas Edison put it this way, "Being busy does not always mean real work. The object of all work is production or accomplishment and to either of these ends there must be forethought, system, planning, intelligence, and honest purpose, as well as perspiration. Seeming to do is not doing."[4]

Three Enemies of Intentionality

There's an adage that says, "If what you are doing is not working, try a new or different approach." So if your good intentions are not translating into meaningful productivity, it's time to find out why. There are enemies out there seeking to derail you from maximum productivity. You don't have to look very far to find them. Some of these little termites eat away at the foundation of your life, and when you try to build on the foundation that you thought was solid, it collapses into a pile of rubble.

One more thing before we look at the enemies of intentionality—not all enemies are equal, some have more power than others to affect you. Before we can turn our "good intentions" into "intentionality," let's consider my top three enemies.

Enemy 1: Making a list and checking it twice—Goal Setting

Now before your brain explodes, let me say I am not against setting goals or making a to-do list. Not at all. But, a good thing becomes a dangerous thing when we think that merely writing down goals on a piece of paper is the same as taking action to accomplish those goals.

Tips on goal setting:

Make your goals line up.

I don't know how many times I have started my year with two pages of goals to accomplish. Every morning I would look over the list, like looking at a police lineup, all spread out shoulder to shoulder. Before I knew it, I was overwhelmed and ready to toss the whole thing. I learned a valuable lesson. I started making my goals line up in front of me, single file, and that way, I could only see what was first in line. I started a system whereby to maximize the process—I would only write down one goal per sheet of paper. That way, I stopped myself from looking ahead, and I could concentrate on one goal at a time. Work out your own system. You don't have to stop making goals, but don't become a slave to them either.

Make the easiest stand in front.

When it comes to goal setting, there are as many opinions as there are "experts" who tell you the best way to do it. Some say to start with the hardest and work your way to the easiest. Others will say to do the opposite. Keep in mind the issue is productivity with results, not just being busy, right? I make the easiest goal to stand in front of me first. Why? Taking the easy guy first will give me instant satisfaction and spur me to tackle the next goal in line.

No jumping the line, please!

Nobody likes a line jumper. How does that apply to goal setting? The temptation is to look ahead and see if I can tackle more than one at a time, even allowing goals to "jump the line." This can cause all kinds of disruption and confusion; so if you are tempted, just say NO!

> What we need is a simple yet effective way to take actions that will get us where we want to go. Gaining on our goals must be done incrementally, little by little, one step at a time.
>
> —RANDY CARLSON[5]

Enemy 2: Jack of all trades and master of none—Multitasking

The apostle Paul said, *"Brothers and sisters, I do not consider myself yet to have taken hold of it. But one thing I do: Forgetting what is behind and straining toward what is ahead"* (Philippians 3:13 NIV).

Paul would not subscribe to the idea of being a "Jack of all trades and master of none." On the contrary, he could have never accomplished what he did if he took the approach of many leaders today who brag about being multitaskers. Paul was instrumental in the founding of many churches and wrote 75 percent of the New Testament. I dare say he could not have accomplished as much if he had been a multitasker, instead of focusing on *"one thing."*

Two Common Myths of the Multitasker

1. I thought I could get more done.

I don't know how many times I have heard multitaskers say that they get more done than the average person. There is only one thing wrong with that assessment—it's wrong!

> Multitasking is a lie. It's a lie because nearly everyone accepts it as an effective thing to do. It's become so mainstream that people actually think it's something they should do, and do as often as possible.
>
> —GARY KELLER[6]

Multitaskers often miss out on the joy of a completed project. Why? It is only because they mistakenly think that by engaging more than one thing at a time, more will be completed. The result is often disappointment, discouragement, and defeat.

> Clifford Nass, a Stanford professor whose pioneering research into how humans interact with technology found that the increasingly screen-saturated, multitasking modern world was not nurturing the ability to concentrate, analyze or feel empathy. Yet when it comes to managing irresistible new technologies, people tell themselves they are prepared. Denial is a great enabler, Dr. Nass found. One of his most publicized research projects was a 2009 study on multitasking. He and his colleagues presumed that people who frequently juggled computer, phone or

television screens, or just different applications, would be skilled at ignoring irrelevant information, or able to switch between tasks efficiently, or possessed of a particularly orderly memory. He added, "One would think that if people were bad at multitasking, they would stop. However, when we talk with the multitaskers, they seem to think they're great at it and seem totally unfazed and totally able to do more and more and more."[7]

2. I thought I could focus on more than one thing at a time.

Not being able to focus on more than one thing at a time is the reason why driving and texting is against the law in most if not all states. Many deadly accidents have occurred because drivers were reading their emails or texting a friend. I found out the hard way the importance of focus. I was driving down the interstate and looked over to observe a roadside sign advertising a vegetable market. As I was reading the sign, I suddenly realized the car drifting toward what I was reading, and it almost caused me to crash. My focus was on the sign not on the highway, and my inattention could have been deadly.

Yes, we can indeed *do* more than one thing at a time, such as listening to music while mowing the lawn. But the fact remains that the brain is not wired to *focus* on more than one thing at a time.

> Multitasking is merely the opportunity to screw up more than one thing at a time.
>
> —STEVE UZZELL[8]

Enemy 3: *Making the wrong choice—between the good and the best*

Every morning we start our day by making choices. From morning till night, our lives are nothing more than a string of endless options. Choices such as: What do I wear to the office today? What should I eat for lunch? Should I cancel the meeting?

"Putting first things first is an issue at the very heart of life," says Stephen R. Covey in his best-selling book, *First Things First*. Covey adds, "Decisions are easier when it's a question of 'good' or 'bad.' We can easily see how some ways we could spend our time are wasteful, mind-numbing, even destructive. But for most of us, the issue is not between the 'good' and the 'bad,' but between the 'good' and the 'best.' So often, the enemy of the best is the good."[9]

Making the right choices that lead to productive habits is the key to intentional living. Whether we want to admit it or not, we are the sum total of the choices we make, good or bad. The old saying, "The road to hell is paved with good intentions," speaks of someone who is putting off the questions of eternity. But in the context of living a life of fulfillment, it could be stated another way: "The road to failure and a life of frustration and defeat is paved with good intentions."

Our future is determined not by some great event that shakes us out of our mundane routine, but by small daily choices. As Covey observed, "by choosing the best over the good, our choices become seeds that will sprout and grow into a life worth living."

The words of Eleanor Roosevelt ring true: One's philosophy is not best expressed in words. It is expressed in the choices one makes. In the long run, we shape our lives and we shape ourselves. The process never ends until we die. And the choices we make are ultimately our responsibility.

—TIM KIMMEL[10]

Top Three Qualities of an *Intentional* Leader

1. *Intentional leaders take one day at a time.*

You know the answer to the question, "How do you eat an elephant?" right? One bite at a time! Intentional leaders know that dreams and goals will not be reached in a day or even a month. It is in taking the small steps, the "one bite at a time" principle, that takes them to their destination. Years ago, gospel singer Cristy Lane put those very sentiments in her famous song, *"One Day at a Time."*

> One day at a time, sweet Jesus
>
> That's all I'm asking from You
>
> Just give me the strength to do every day
>
> What I have to do
>
> Yesterday's gone, sweet Jesus
>
> And tomorrow may never be mine
>
> Lord, help me today, show me the way
>
> One day at a time[11]

Don't start your day without a plan of action.

Around 1994-95, Microsoft launched an ad campaign touting the personal computer. The tag line was simple: "What do you want to do today?" The implication was, whatever you want to do our computers will guide you. Sounds pretty simple, doesn't it? The same simple logic could be applied to us. What is the one thing you want to accomplish today? What is the "one bite of the elephant" you can take today that will make you feel that you have taken a step toward intentional living?

Don't allow discouragement to derail you.

Everyone deals with discouragement at some point. No one is immune. Period. When you make up your mind to become intentional about your life, I can almost guarantee that at some point you will be challenged on your commitment. It's not a matter of if, but when; it's going to happen, so be prepared.

Remember King David? He was the one who took down Goliath and became known as the worshipping warrior. But even a giant killer gets discouraged. Without going into the details, suffice it to say that First Samuel Chapter 30 tells us about the time David came home and found the city burned to the ground, and his family taken hostage. Not only that, his men wanted to stone him for being a lousy leader. Wow! Now that's what I call a bad day.

What did David do when he was discouraged? The Bible tells us, *"David was greatly distressed because the men were talking of stoning him; each one was bitter in spirit because of his sons and daughters. But David found strength in the Lord his God"* (1 Samuel 30:6). David turned to the only One who could give him the wisdom and strength to carry on.

If you find yourself having the "David" kind of day when everything is falling apart, it is time to turn to the Lord who promises to gives you the courage to keep going. Remember, God promised that what He started in you He will complete. Even though others may want to "stone you," God will not leave you hanging by a thread while your detractors hold the scissors!

Don't allow others to become more passionate about your life than you are!

Passion means an "Ardent affection: love...a strong liking for or devotion to some activity, object or concept." There is one thing I am sure of—I must never allow others to be more passionate about my life than I am. How can you tell if you are allowing this in your life? Ask yourself a few questions:

- Do I always have to be prodded to do things I already know to do?
- Do I fizzle out before reaching the finish line of any project?
- Do I spend more time feeling guilty about past wrong choices than making future right choices?
- Do I accept responsibility for my future, but I'm unwilling to take action to get there?

If you answered yes to these questions, it's a good bet that you have lost your passion and zeal to transform your life into one of intentionality. Fulfilling your purpose requires passion—zeal, fervency, or enthusiasm. *Purpose* has to do with our head, thinking right about why we're here and understanding our calling. *Passion* has to do with our heart, the internal fire that motivates us and energizes us to fulfill our purpose and do God's will. God is the Source of spiritual passion. The Holy Spirit comes to ignite us with holy fire.

In the world we live in, natural passion is often a key to success and impact. Knowing information is valuable, but possessing the fire is invaluable. Nothing major in history was ever accomplished without zeal. It is the deciding difference between successful and unsuccessful people in every field of endeavor. The fire inside affects everything on the outside. William Ward says, "Enthusiasm and persistence can make an average person superior; indifference and lethargy can make a superior person average."[12]

Passion is not static; it doesn't stay the same. A fire either spreads or burns out. The tendency of fire, if left alone, is to go out. Passion works the same way. We need to work it, stoke it, and build it. Once the fire goes out, another enemy that is always lurking in the shadows will begin to worm its way into our heart. That enemy is apathy. Apathy isn't a mental condition; it is a condition of the heart.

> Discover your divine assignment and you have no reason to retreat. Discover your passion and you laugh in the face of defeat.
>
> —KIRK NUGENT[13]

2. *Intentional leaders are not afraid to take ownership.*

Taking ownership or responsibility is a key trait of intentional leaders. Intentional leaders never look for the easy way out, but rather demonstrate ownership over every aspect of their lives. No matter the issues at hand, responsible people do not shy away from taking all necessary steps to ensure things are taken care of, which is called getting the job done no matter what it takes.

> Responsibility is a unique concept…. You may share it with others, but your portion is not diminished. You may delegate it, but it is still with you…. If responsibility is rightfully yours, no evasion, or ignorance or passing the blame can shift the burden to someone else. Unless you can point your finger at the man who is responsible when something goes wrong, then you have never had anyone really responsible.[14]

Taking ownership means refusing to allow others to fall on their swords.

Falling into the trap of asking someone else to fall on the sword may make your self-indulgent pity party more interesting, but it will not solve the problem. The bottom line—the only one who can make a difference in your life is *you*. Period! If you want things to change, then take steps to change whatever needs changing and stop all the finger pointing. Because when *everyone* is responsible, *no one* is responsible. Responsibility is a *me,* not a *we* activity.

> We demand corporate responsibility for a shoddy product or a polluted beach, however, we refused to require individuals to except responsibility for their acts of irresponsible behavior. Perhaps it is easier to legislate and regulate spoiled meat than it is to legislate or regulate spoiled people—whether they are from the west side of Chicago or the president of the savings and loan.[15]

Taking ownership means finishing what you start.

Responsibility is defined as "a state of being reliable, dependable, accountable, answerable and trustworthy." I add to that definition: responsibility is responding to your ability. Responsibility also involves entering into a contract or an obligation. All of these terms indicate the transfer of something valuable. The implication is that the receiver of the trust is to achieve some positive result. Responsibility also embraces self-reliance, effectiveness, faithfulness, and capability. In essence, responsibility is *the ability to respond.* Each time we fulfill a responsibility, there comes with it peace and contentment that is rewarding and personally satisfying.

3. *Intentional leaders have learned the fine art of saying, "No!"*

In 1986, First Lady Nancy Reagan introduced to the American public her "Just Say No" campaign. The campaign was her effort to raise the public's awareness of the danger of drug use. The results were mixed at best, but the idea of learning to say "No" was forever implanted in my brain.

Great leaders know they can't say yes to everything and everybody.

We want to please everybody, don't we? And if we start saying no to certain things, we are afraid that we will get the reputation of being a loner, cold, or worse yet, uncaring. Here's something I have learned, and it wasn't easy—learning to say no is the best thing I have ever done!

> The art of saying yes is by default, the art of saying no. Saying yes to everyone is the same as yes to nothing. Each additional obligation chips away at your effectiveness at everything you try. So the more things you do, the less successful you are at any one of them. You can't please everyone, so don't try. In fact, when you try, the one person you absolutely won't please is yourself.[16]

Great leaders know that by saying "no" new boundaries are being set.

If we ever have any hope of becoming intentional in what we are called to do, we have to set certain boundaries, and learning to say no helps us to do just that. We set boundaries with our children, pets, and even our neighbors, and we need to learn how to fix certain limits with those with whom we work. Learning to say no may not win you a popularity contest in your organization, but it will keep you from the stress of taking on more than you should.

Great leaders know that to go big, you have to stay small.

Nike CEO, Mark Parker says that shortly after becoming CEO, he talked to Steve Jobs on the phone. "Do you have any advice?" Parker asked Jobs. Here is what Jobs had to say: Nike makes some of the best products in the world. Products that you lust after. But you also make a lot of crap. Just get rid of the crappy stuff and focus on the good stuff.

"He was absolutely right," said Parker. "We had to edit," Jobs followed this very advice himself back in 1998 when he shrunk Apple's product line from 350 to 10. So instead of creating 350 crappy products, or 200 mediocre products, or 100 good products Apple focused on creating 10 incredibly designed products.

The lesson here is that if your ultimate goal is to produce outstanding work, no matter which industry you're in, you must be comfortable with the fact that most of the work you produce you'll have to throw out. Jobs says it best: People think focus means saying yes to the thing you've got to focus on. But that's not what it means at all. It means saying no to the hundred other good ideas that there are. You have to pick carefully. I'm actually as proud of the things we haven't done as the things I have done. Innovation is saying "no" to 1,000 things.[17]

Or as a great leader friend of mine says, "Snip snip," get your scissors out!

A Final Thought

Jesus Christ was the most intentional leader who ever lived. His leadership ability is a model of consistency, and we would all be better served to learn from His example. Jesus was the ultimate leader who knew that to go big, He had to stay small.

- On occasion, Jesus spoke to multitudes, but speaking to large crowds was not His main focus.

- He spent most of His time with the twelve men He handpicked for personal discipleship.

- He grew His base to include seventy who were trained and mobilized to carry His message.

- Of the twelve and the seventy, He only shared His most intimate moments with His inner circle of Peter, James, and John.

Jesus's intentional strategy was different and yet highly effective. He set new standards for how to grow from the ground up—not the top down. Read the book of Acts, and you will discover that by employing this simple, stay-small strategy, He shifted the paradigm that allowed a handful of disciples to turn the world upside down!

9

GREAT LEADERS CROSS THE FINISH LINE FROM THE BEGINNING

Do you see someone skilled in their work? They will serve before kings; they will not serve before officials of low rank.

—PROVERBS 22:29

The practice of perseverance is the discipline of the noblest virtues. To run well, we must run to the end. It is not the fighting but the conquering that gives a hero his title to renown.

—ELIAS LYMAN MAGOON[1]

Introduction

Merriam-Webster's online dictionary says that *diligent* is characterized by steady, earnest, and energetic effort: PAINSTAKING.

What comes to mind when you consider the word *diligence*? Does your subconscious automatically search through your mental files and throw up an image of a friend, or a coworker you consider stubborn as a mule? Sadly, we often think that when a person is diligent, they are close-minded, driven, or just plain difficult. Some or all of that may be true because successful leaders are sometimes viewed as task-oriented to the point of ignoring distractions.

I have learned that successful leaders are willing to do things that unsuccessful leaders refuse to do—mainly, they stay at whatever task is in front of them until the job is complete.

One of the most famous illustrations of the "I will not quit attitude" is the story about the race between the tortoise and the hare. It has all the elements you want in a classic underdog story. In this simple childhood fable, we can learn the secret of winning every race we enter, no matter our skill level.

Let me share it with you now...by the way, the outcome is always the same!

> There once was a speedy hare who bragged about how fast he could run. Tired of hearing him boast, Slow and Steady, the tortoise, challenged him to a race. All the animals in the forest gathered to watch.
>
> Hare ran down the road for a while and then paused to rest. He looked back at Slow and Steady and cried out, "How do you expect to win this race when you are walking along at your slow, slow pace?"
>
> Hare stretched himself out alongside the road and fell asleep, thinking, "There is plenty of time to relax."
>
> Slow and Steady walked and walked. He never, ever stopped until he came to the finish line.

The animals who were watching cheered so loudly for Tortoise, they woke up Hare.

Hare stretched and yawned and began to run again, but it was too late. Tortoise was over the line.

After that, Hare always reminded himself, "Don't brag about your lightning pace, for Slow and Steady won the race!"[2]

Looking at the two competitors, you can observe two different leadership styles or attitudes. Of the two, which one do you more closely identify with, the speedy hare or slow and steady tortoise?

First: Speedy Hare.

- He thought he had all the skill and speed needed to win the race. So, why bother to work on improving his skills; after all, he probably won tougher races before.

- He developed the classic, "I can coast along, so there is no need to get passionate about it" attitude.

- He decided he could win with minimal effort. He already declared himself the winner.

- He made the mistake of underestimating his competition.

- When he realized his mistake, it was too late to make up for lost time.

Second: Slow and Steady Tortoise

- He was diligent and kept going even though he knew he had lesser talent.

- He ran his own race and wasn't bothered by how fast the other guy was.

- He wasn't distracted and didn't listen to the noise of the crowd.

- He stayed focused on the finish line.

- He used his motivation to win and stayed with his game plan of "slow and steady wins the race" every time!

In one of the greatest upsets in racing history, the Tortoise beat the Hare, and it wasn't even close. The overriding lesson is clear: *You don't have to be the fastest, the most skilled, or the most naturally talented person on the planet to succeed. All you need to do is take the skill you have and refuse to give up or give in, even when others don't think you can win.*

In the world of sports, there have been plenty of upsets. Whether it was the New York Jets defeat of the Baltimore Colts in Super Bowl III, or the stunning victory by the USA Hockey Team's defeat of the Soviet Union in the 1980 Olympic games, forever known as the "Miracle on Ice."

One of the lesser-known, yet most captivating upsets took place in the 1964 Olympic Games in Tokyo, Japan. His name was Billy Mills. He ran in the 10,000-meter race. No one expected him to even qualify; and if he did, he certainly could not beat the best in the world.

Only one man believed that he could win.

That person? Billy Mills himself.

The following is the account of race as told by Ben Chodos:

> At the 1964 games in Tokyo, he made it to the finals of the 10,000m race but was still just an unknown runner in a heat of 29 athletes.

However, when the final laps started to approach, Mills was right there with Australia's Ron Clarke, the world record-holder at the time. The two were joined by Tunisia's Mohammed Gammoudi.

Clarke's record was nearly a minute faster than Mills' qualifying time, but it was Gammoudi who made the decisive move down the stretch.

The Tunisian ran in between Clarke and Mills, nudging the two runners out of way and opening a narrow lead.

Clarke began to close the gap, with Mills close behind in third place. Just when the race seemed to be narrowed down to Gammoudi and Clarke, Mills shifted into another gear and sprinted by his competition in the final 100 meters of the race.

Mills later said that his vision was coming and going down the final stretch, and he just kept telling himself that he could win over and over again.

In the same interview, Mills identified the motivation behind his monumental effort: *"That one fleeting moment you know that you're the very best in the world."* ...Mills understood and channeled that spirit more than anyone ever has and he used it to push himself to unimaginable heights.[3]

It was diligence that won the race between the tortoise and the hare. It was diligence that enabled Billy Mills to win against the fastest runners in the world. And, it is diligence that will give you the edge and help you win every race you enter, no matter how strong or skilled your competition.

Three Amazing Facts About Diligence

Fact 1. Diligence Is a Skill

People will use all kinds of excuses as to why they are not successful. One of the most popular reasons is that people believe successful leaders are naturally endowed with a diligent spirit. In other words, some people were just born to work hard, finish every task, and win every race. Not true!

In his book, *The Richest Man Who Ever Lived,* Steven K. Scott wrote:

> Diligence is a learnable skill that combines: creative persistence, a smart working effort rightly planned and rightly performed in a timely, efficient, and effective manner to attain a result that is pure and of the highest quality of excellence.[4]

Diligence is not a gift of the Spirit or just a personality trait. No, diligence is a learnable skill. Therefore, you don't learn diligence by attending seminars, reading a *Time-Life* book, or staying at a Holiday Inn Express! Maybe some of those things might help to get you started, but it's like any other skill—it takes time and effort to apply its principles.

How does a person learn the skill of diligence? You learn diligence and persistence the same way you would walk a mile. One foot in front of the other. It's the same with learning the skill of diligence; you take one step at a time. I might suggest using the PMF plan of attack:

P—*Plan your strategy.* If you want to find out why most people are not successful, ask a straightforward question: *Do you start each task with a focused plan of attack, or do you shoot from the hip?* I'll let you decide which one is the most popular. I'm sure you know the old saying, "If you fail to plan, you are planning to fail!"

Planning your strategy to tackle any task must always involve careful *time management.* If you don't manage your time, your time will manage you. Just think of how much we could accomplish if we didn't waste so much time. Proverbs 21:5 (MSG) tells us, *"Careful planning puts you ahead in the long run; hurry and scurry puts you further behind."*

M—*Motivate yourself, and stop depending on others to keep you going.* As a child, I needed some motivation to do certain chores. I don't ever remember carrying out the trash or cleaning my room without first a not-so-gentle reminder by my mother telling me, at least ten times, to do so.

As adults, we should not need someone to prop us up to keep us from falling over when it comes to our daily, weekly, or monthly responsibilities. If you lack motivation, it could be because you have lost your desire for something better than what you have. If you want something you've never had, you have to be willing to do things you've never done—and that takes a dose of inspiration, backed up by a truckload of self-motivation. My motivation is simply that no one wants me to succeed more than me.

You're more likely to be diligent about something if you love doing it. The etymology of *diligent* reflects the fact that affection can lead to energetic effort. According the Merriam-Webster.com, the word *diligent,* which entered English in the 14th century by way of Anglo-French, descends from the Latin verb *diligere,* meaning "to value or esteem highly" or "to love." Of course, you don't need to care for the task at hand in order to be diligent, but it certainly does help!

And I say often that I love what I do—and love with whom I do it!

F—*Finish what you start.* Have you ever started a task only to be confronted by roadblocks that caused you to quit? Sure, we all have. The key is to begin with the attitude of no matter what obstacles are in my way, I will finish the task, period!

> Diligence, by its very definition, is the application of focused and persistent effort to complete a task. The diligent person has an extra edge to put in more dedicated hours towards realizing their goal, and that becomes the deciding factor for their extraordinary success in life.[5]

The great apostle Paul developed the heart of a finisher. At the end of his life, he wrote a letter to his son in the faith. In Second Timothy 4:6-7, he says, *"For I am already being poured out like a drink offering, and the time for my departure is near. I have fought the good fight, I have finished the race, I have kept the faith."*

I have no doubt there were times when Paul wanted to throw up his hands and walk away from his assignment. If you read his resume, alongside his accomplishments, you will discover he faced some of the most intense challenges any leader could endure (see Second Corinthians 11:22-33). Why didn't he quit? Paul knew, more than most of us, that a leader is judged more by how he finishes the race, than how he started. You don't build a lasting legacy by standing at the starting line. You leave a legacy by crossing the finishing line!

Paul kept his eye on the prize and refused to give up or give in to the temptation to withdraw from his God-given mission. Again, Philippians 3:13-14 tells us his philosophy:

*Brothers and sisters, I do not consider myself yet to have taken hold of it. But one thing **I do**: Forgetting what is behind and straining toward what is ahead, **I press on** toward the goal to win the prize for which God has called me heavenward in Christ Jesus.*

Fact 2. *Diligence Is a Two-Sided Coin*

If diligence is on one side of the coin, what's the other side? It's none other than the faithful friend to all successful leaders—*persistence!* Yes, diligence and persistence are two sides of the same coin, and one without the other is incomplete.

The best definition to describe the difference between the two traits says, "As adjectives, the difference between diligent and persistent is that diligent is performing with intense concentration, focus, responsible regard, while persistent is obstinately refusing to give up or let go."[6]

Diligence looks at the task with *intense concentration* and plans out the attack. Persistence leans in and whispers in diligence's ear and says, "We are going to finish this task no matter what it takes!"

If you consider all the great leaders of the past, one leadership trait is common among them—persistence. The leaders who stand out refused to give up or give in. In most cases, it was not their gifts, talents, or skill—it's the fact they merely lasted longer than the competition!

If I had to choose my favorite leader of the 20th century, it would have to be Sir Winston Churchill. I am convinced that without his courage, World War II would have had a different outcome. His leadership style, often criticized and ridiculed, was what kept Great Britain from collapsing under the weight of the Nazi boot. Churchill was the epitome of a persistent and diligent leader who used his bulldog attitude as a bulwark against tyranny, and thus saved the Western World.

In one of his most famous speeches to the House of Commons, in 1940 Churchill declared at the end of his speech:

> ...we shall not flag or fail. We shall go on to the end, we shall fight in France, we shall fight on the seas and oceans, we shall fight with growing confidence and growing strength in the air, we shall defend our Island, whatever the cost may be, we shall fight on the beaches, we shall fight on the landing grounds, we shall fight in the fields and in the streets, we shall fight in the hills; we shall never surrender, and even if, which I do not for a moment believe, this Island or a large part of it were subjugated and starving, then our Empire beyond the seas, armed and guarded by the British Fleet, would carry on the struggle, until, in God's good time, the New World, with all its power and might, steps forth to the rescue and the liberation of the Old.[7]

Fact 3. Diligence Brings Benefits

When it comes to the bottom line, we can practice diligence and reap the benefits, or we can choose to ignore the discipline that diligence requires and realize the negative consequences.

Solomon, the wisest and richest man who ever lived, listed some of the benefits of a life of diligence and perseverance in the book of Proverbs. In the following section, Solomon's insights are cited, as well as my own.

Top Three Benefits of Diligence

1. Diligence gives you an advantage in every situation you face.

> *The **plans of the diligent lead surely to advantage**, but everyone who is hasty comes surely to poverty* (Proverbs 21:5 NASB).

When I speak of having an advantage, I do not mean an "unfair" advantage, but what we used to call a "leg up" on the competition. Show me a leader who is diligent in their plans, combined with a strong commitment to hard work, and I'll show you a leader who is walking into every situation with an advantage!

> How you start is important, very important, but in the end, it is how you finish that counts. It is easier to be a self-starter than a self-finisher. The victor in the race is not the one who dashes off swiftest but the one who leads at the finish. In the race for success, speed is less important than stamina. The sticker outlasts the sprinter in life's race. In America, we breed many hares but not so many tortoises.[8]

2. Diligence brings material blessings.

> *In all labor there is profit, but mere talk leads only to poverty* (Proverbs 14:23 NASB).

Anything worth having is worth working for, and that includes every aspect of our lives. Solomon is clear—talk is cheap and hard work is what brings benefits, not the least of which is material blessings. Reaping the benefits of diligence and perseverance may not happen overnight. But the promise of reward is to those who will not give up at the first sign of obstacles.

> Diligence is like an investment, which means that what you put into something determines what you will get out of it. A diligent person works hard because anything worth doing is worth doing right, and the way you do your work is a reflection of who you are.[9]

3. Diligence insulates you from following after failures.

> *He who cultivates his land will have plenty of bread, but he who follows worthless people and frivolous pursuits will have plenty of poverty* (Proverbs 28:19 AMP).

One of the greatest dangers successful leaders face is allowing lazy, unproductive people into their sphere of influence. If you are going to follow after someone, make sure they know where they are going. If you hang around people who have no vision or passion, you will likely end up in the same ditch.

> Keep on going, and the chances are that you will stumble on something, perhaps when you are least expecting it. I never heard of anyone ever stumbling on something sitting down.
>
> —CHARLES F. KETTERING[10]

The Secret of Diligence from the Lowly Ant

When talking about how to learn the skill of diligence, Solomon takes us out into a forest and points to an anthill. He says that the ant is the essence of hard work and diligence. We would be wise to observe and learn the ants' secret. If you want to learn how to incorporate diligence into your life, maybe it's time to do what the Bible says in Proverbs 6:9-11 (MSG).

> *You lazy fool, look at an ant. Watch it closely; let it teach you a thing or two. Nobody has to tell it what to do. All summer it stores up food; at harvest it stockpiles provisions. So how long are you going to laze around doing nothing? How long before you get out of bed? A nap here, a nap there, a day off here, a day off there, sit back, take it easy—do you know what comes next? Just this: You can look forward to a dirt-poor life, poverty your permanent houseguest!*

It would be impossible to sit down and talk to an ant, I will grant you that. But let's use our imaginations for a moment and allow the AIC (Ant In Charge) to teach us *three valuable lessons about diligence.*

Lesson 1: We believe in hard work and won't tolerate laziness.

You won't find lazy ants sitting around waiting for the clock to tell them it's time to go home. Hard work is a sign of diligence. You will never see an ant taking time off for some personal time. And, you won't find an ant looking at a brochure to see where to vacation next year. There is nothing wrong with downtime or vacations, but it seems that some in our current culture are more interested in how little they can do and still get by. The ant is willing to do whatever it takes to provide for himself and his ant-mates!

I've read that:

- An ant may carry up to 50X its own weight.
- In a single summer, a large colony may excavate 30,000-40,000 pounds of earth to make its nest.

- An ant may make as many as four trips a day to a food source which may be over 400 feet from the nest. A rough equivalent to our walking 68 miles.

- Ants use the sun's position as a reference for navigation. By walking in a direction that keeps the sun at the same angle, the ant is able to walk in a straight line. If covered by a box and later released, he will deviate from his course by the same angle that the sun moved.[11]

Lesson 2: We are self-starters—we don't need a boss.

Solomon says *nobody* has to tell the ant what to do. If you want a definition of a self-starter, that would be it! The ant can do its work without a boss, a leader, or someone standing on his shoulder watching every move he makes.

According to Dan Charney, President of Direct Recruiters, Inc., "A big deal is being made about self-starters these days because it is at the top of a hiring manager's list. It's considered one of the key traits that employers are looking for in their employees. However, in the real world, most people are not self-starters. We don't always live up to expectations or our own ambitions. But that doesn't mean we can't change and become a self-starter."[12]

Lesson 3: We are diligent to plan for the future.

Ants are so focused on their mission to prepare for the future that they know, even without a boss telling them, that wintertime is coming and if they don't prepare, they will die. *"All summer it stores up food; at harvest it stockpiles provisions."*

If the ant decided it wasn't essential to plan, his lack of vision for the future would lead to disaster. Proverbs 29:18 tells us, *"Where there is no revelation, people cast off restraint; but blessed is the one who heeds wisdom's instruction."* In other words, the ant works hard and is motivated by a clear vision of what needs to be done, to thrive as well as survive.

When we live with a plan to accomplish our vision, we find that diligence keeps us on the right track to see the fulfillment of that dream.

A Final Thought

Diligence is a skill to learn and a choice to make. You can achieve any goal you set before your eyes, but it takes time and a daily commitment to develop the habit of diligence and persistence. When it comes to being diligent and winning in life, *choose to be slow and steady every time!*

Entrepreneurs have all these qualities. But more than possessing the qualities, they practice them. I compensate all of my staff very well. No hourly wages, only salaries. Why? Because I expect from myself and them a 24/7, 365 commitment to who we are and those we serve. While the hours we labor in a day may be limited, our commitments are not.

10

GREAT LEADERS VALUE INTEGRITY OVER CELEBRITY

The integrity of the upright guides them, but the unfaithful are destroyed by their duplicity.

—PROVERBS 11:3

If you have integrity, nothing else matters. If you don't have integrity, nothing else matters.

—ALAN K. SIMPSON[1]

Introduction

Hardly a day passes without seeing the word *crisis* splashed across the television or a news computer screen. In recent years, we have been warned about crises including: oil, money, Middle East, constitutional, climate change, and on and on it goes. With each passing day, a new emergency pops up. But take comfort, if you don't like today's crisis, there will surely be a new one tomorrow!

There is one crisis that stands head and shoulders above the rest, and yet it is mostly ignored—the *integrity crisis*. In my estimation, many of the so-called crises we are facing could be eliminated. How? By understanding that without integrity, we are nothing more than a society built on lies, false hope, and deception. The "ends justify the means" mentality is crippling our homes, our businesses, and yes, even our churches.

No segment of society has been immune from the breakdown of integrity, character, and trustworthiness. From Wall Street to Main Street, and from the boardroom to the living room, the crack in our moral foundation is obvious.

Our political system has become so corrupt that it's almost impossible for someone to keep their integrity intact. It's like the old joke that pictures two people standing in front of a gravestone that reads: *"Here lies an honest man, and a great politician."* One person looks at the other and declares, *"Look, they started burying two people in the same grave now!"* It would be funnier if it were not so true!

Great leaders know if we don't place value on integrity, everything will collapse into chaos. It has been said that everything rises and falls on leadership. That statement may be accurate, but I submit to you that in fact, everything rises and falls on integrity. There are too many examples of very influential leaders without integrity who destroy rather than build. So, everything rises on the right kind of leadership, and falls on the wrong!

Amy Rees Anderson writes:

> If I could teach only one value to live by, it would be this: Success will come and go, but integrity is forever. Integrity means doing the right thing at all times and in all circumstances, whether or not anyone is watching. It takes having the courage to do the right thing, no matter what the consequences will be. Building a reputation of

integrity takes years, but it takes only a second to lose, so never allow yourself to ever do anything that would damage your integrity.[2]

Five Things Integrity Is *Not*

1. Integrity is not blowing smoke.

Blowing smoke is a common term used to describe someone who is not very trustworthy. They love to talk—blow smoke—and come across as insincere and empty. When you blow smoke on people, you are trying to cover up something that you don't want people to see. And it's usually something made up to sound important, exaggerated, or just a flat-out lie. You can only "smoke over" lack of integrity for so long. Eventually, people will stop listening or caring about what you have to say.

The underlying meaning of the word *integrity* is wholeness or completeness, or being undivided. A person of integrity is someone whose words and actions line up. They don't say one thing and do something different.

Dr. Dave Martin observed:

Integrity lies at the very heart of greatness and leadership because everything you will ever do revolves around who you are on the inside. Who you are on the inside is demonstrated every day by your actions, the things you do, and the words you speak. Therefore, successful people and particularly great leaders are characterized by honesty, trustworthiness, and dealing straight with every person they encounter, no matter the situation.[3]

2. *Integrity is not handing out empty envelopes.*

One year in a political campaign, the party in power used a very catchy slogan to promote its run for a second term: *"Promises made, Promises kept!"* I'm not sure I am up on all the promises that were made. I am reasonably sure that if some of the promises were not kept the media would have been reporting it night and day.

Every time we make a promise, we are stuffing that promise in an envelope to be opened at the appropriate time. It is kind of like an IOU. One of the most glaring failures a parent can make is handing out empty envelopes to their kids. I'm sure I'm not the only parent who has raised their children to never to make a promise they don't intend to keep.

The failure to follow through with a promise is a direct reflection on the character of the one who made it. Everything we do is a reflection of those promises we have made to ourselves and others. To hand out empty envelopes is putting our integrity at risk.

3. *Integrity is not wearing "two faces" at the same time.*

One day Jesus was speaking to a group of religious leaders. This was not some ordinary group—they were the leading religious leaders of the day. I'm sure they never expected Jesus to call them out, but that is what He did. (You can read the full story in Matthew 23.) Jesus used one particular word to describe their behavior, *hypocrites.* These so-called leaders, not unlike some today, were the opposite of living lives of integrity.

The original meaning of the word *hypocrite* means an actor or someone who is playing a part in a stage play. So, hypocrites are people who are not what they claim to be, and they are capable of wearing two faces at the same time!

A hypocrite is "willing to adapt themselves often in dramatic ways to win approval. They are willing to play many roles and wear many masks to give the audience what they want. They are like actors on a stage, who seek applause or perhaps laughter and approval."[4]

One of my favorite movies is *One-Eyed Jacks*. It's a Western starring Marlon Brando and Karl Malden. Malden plays a crook-turned-sheriff. In one scene, Brando says to Malden, "You're a one eyed jack around here, but I've seen the other side of your face." Eventually, without integrity, everyone will see that other eye!

4. *Integrity is not found at the local Jiffy Lube.*

One of the selling points of the local Jiffy Lube is the claim to change your vehicle's oil in fifteen minutes or less. What a novel concept. Changing your oil or cooking a hot dog in a microwave may work well in our "Give it to me now" culture, but it won't work when it comes to forming a lifetime of integrity.

Integrity is not formed overnight—rather in the daily pressure cooker of life. Each day we are given the opportunity to make wise decisions. Each decision we make adds more building blocks of a solid foundation of character and integrity that can withstand the howling winds of temptation. The apostle Paul says in Romans 5:3-4, *"Not only so, but we also glory in our sufferings, because we know that suffering produces perseverance; perseverance, character; and character, hope."*

> Character is shaped by the challenges of life, including both the victories and the defeats that result from life's challenges. But character is more than the challenges themselves and it is more than the outcome of the challenges. Character is the sum total of the mental and

ethical traits that a man develops as a result of walking through life's difficulties.[5]

5. Integrity is not winning a talent contest.

King Solomon says this about integrity, *"Whoever walks in integrity walks securely, but whoever takes crooked paths will be found out"* (Proverbs 10:9).

There is no more perfect example of Solomon's words than the first king of Israel. He was a handsome man by the name of Saul. He knew a lot about talent, charm, and how to flash a winning smile. The Scripture tells us, *"Kish had a son named Saul, as handsome a young man as could be found anywhere in Israel, and he was a head taller than anyone else"* (1 Samuel 9:2). There isn't a doubt this tall, good-looking guy was the perfect fit for a people who valued talent and charm over character. But while men applaud talent, God applauds character.

It only took two years for the cracks in Saul's character to be exposed. His disobedience to the clear command of God cost him his reputation, his kingdom, and eventually his life. The moral of the story—our charm and character will only carry us only so far. At the end of the day, what is inside us will be exposed. When Saul felt the pressure to make the right decision, he flunked the test. His lack of integrity was revealed for the world to see by his deception. (Read First Samuel 15 for the full story.)

You may win a talent contest by fooling your friends. You might think that smooth words and a winning smile will carry you a long way. But in fact, when the pressure is on, the cracks in the foundation called character—your integrity—will be exposed.

When Warren Buffett was asked to share his wisdom about hiring the right people for his company, he said, "Somebody once said that in looking for people to hire, you look for three qualities: integrity, intelligence, and energy. And if you don't have the first, the other two will kill you. You think about it; it's true. If you hire somebody without [integrity], you really want them to be dumb and lazy."[6]

Seven Characteristics of Great Leaders Who Value Integrity

1. Great leaders honor their commitments.

General Douglas MacArthur said, "A true leader has the confidence to stand alone, the courage to make tough decisions, and the compassion to listen to the needs of others. He does not set out to be a leader, but becomes one by the equality of his actions and the *integrity* of his intent."[7]

It has often been said that it takes years of making the right choices and implementing the right actions to make deposits in our integrity bank. And, it only takes one or two bad decisions to make a hefty withdrawal.

> When you have integrity, it will overflow into every relationship, personal and business, and you will be a magnet to attract the right people into your life, for people want to do business with the person who keeps his word.
>
> —NICK UNSWORTH[8]

Ask yourself a few questions to determine where you are on the commitment scale:

- Do I continuously disregard my commitment to show up on time for appointments?

- Am I totally committed to mentor those who are my responsibility?
- Am I committed to speaking the truth even when it's unpopular?
- Am I committed to the vision that God has put in my heart?
- Am I committed to building up my integrity account with everyone in my area of influence?
- Do I mean what I say, and say what I mean?

2. Great leaders call penalties on themselves.

Great leaders are never afraid to recognize and improve their areas of weakness. I like to think of it as calling a penalty on themselves when they know something is wrong. For instance, golf is the only major sport that the players are so bound by the integrity code that they will call a penalty on themselves—even if it costs them a chance of winning. (Chapter 6 cites more details.)

Sportswriter Bob Warters observed:

> In no other sport do the competitors have such a high standard of integrity than in golf. It is still regarded as the bastion of good sportsmanship and the only game where you can call a penalty on yourself. There are no referees waving yellow and red cards, nor officials checking TV replays—apart from when Tiger Woods loses a ball in a clubhouse![9]

There have been occasions where cheating takes place, not only in golf but in other sports as well. But for the most part, the integrity of the game is dependent on the integrity of the individual.

The same is true in our lives. No matter what arena you are in at any given moment, the level of integrity will only rise as high as the individuals present.

3. *Great leaders are the same in public as in private.*

I am reminded of an Old Testament character by the name of Daniel. If you mention his name, most people jump to the Lion's Den story and skip over the early experiences of his life that led up to his amazing deliverance. He didn't become solid, firm, resolute, firmly fixed, and incapable of being diverted from his primary purpose or mission overnight. No, his early formation of integrity led to difficult trials, but with great rewards.

Daniel was a young man, between eighteen and twenty-five, when he was taken captive and shipped off to Babylon. King Nebuchadnezzar had a plan to take the young Hebrew captives, give them the best food, and the best education. The King wanted the wisest and strongest young men possible to lead his nation.

From young Daniel's viewpoint, there was only one thing wrong with the king's plan—if he submitted to the program, it would violate his integrity, and that was not an option. Sure, Daniel could have gone with the flow and justified his actions. He could have said, "I'm far away from home; no one will ever know if I participate or not." He would not have been the first one to say, "I want to fit in, so what's the harm?" He purposed in his heart, not to defile himself with their lifestyle. To eat the king's food might not have looked very serious to others, but to Daniel, it flew in the face of his core values. He chose not to rationalize his actions, and he steadfastly rejected the king's meal plan.

It has been said that what you do when no one is looking is who you really are. A lifestyle of integrity will never allow us to compromise our convictions based on temporary pleasure. If you are not sure about that, ask Daniel! (See the book of Daniel for the full story.)

4. Great leaders know the ends never justify the means.

Simply put, some people think that the result is more important than the means it took to get it. Some people think that it is okay to take actions that are wrong as long as the outcome is worthwhile.

A great leader will never choose to take steps that are flat-out wrong or evil to achieve a specific outcome. The "ends justify the means" philosophy has been around since the beginning of time. It appears that our current society has lifted this false notion that anything goes to a new level of sophistication. What used to be whispered behind the scenes is now spoken of openly, in broad daylight.

A brief sampling shows that every segment of society has been infected:

- *Sports:* It was deemed justified to use Performance Enhancing Drugs (PEDs) to enhance a player's ability to gain the edge. After all, it's about winning the game, not following the rules.

- *Government:* It was considered "necessary" to collect personal and private information on American citizens under the guise of national security, all the while trampling on citizens' rights.

- *Housing Market:* Under the cloak of "we want to help poor people own a home," the mortgage industry cooked up a scheme to get rich by giving sub-prime loans to people who could not afford the monthly payments.

- *Academia:* "The ends justify the means" philosophy was on display when it was revealed that thousands of dollars in bribes were paid to coaches and administrators to gain entrance for wealthy and well-known celebrities' kids into the most prestigious universities in the US.

According to Steven Mintz, PhD:

> The reason the means are important, maybe more important than the ends, is how we get to our goal is just as important as getting there. In other words, destiny tells us what we are to the world, but journey tells who we are; it's the journey that unlocks our potential and establishes who we are as a person and what motivates us towards action.[10]

5. *Great leaders are honest. Period.*

Honesty and integrity go hand in hand. You cannot have one without the other. As leaders, we are often put in situations where quite frankly it would be easier to fudge the truth than to tell all of the truth, all of the time. We can become so fearful that by telling the truth, we will hurt someone's feelings, that we make choices that do not bring about a positive outcome. We might conclude it's not worth the risk—so what do we do?

Let's say a coworker comes to you and asks your honest opinion about a project he or she is working on. You know it's not the person's best work, or even work that others higher up in the chain of command need to see. You have a choice: 1) Tell the truth and risk a friendship; or, 2) lie and let the person think the work is good.

Which one of those two choices would benefit your coworker in the long run? It's not easy, is it?

King Solomon tells us in Proverbs 3:3-4 (NLV):

> *Do not let kindness and truth leave you. Tie them around your neck. Write them upon your heart. So you will find favor and good understanding in the eyes of God and man.*

Solomon makes an interesting observation. He writes that *kindness and truth* should be tied around our necks. I don't think he's telling us to walk around like a celebrity wearing a big sign that hangs on a gold chain around our neck. I take it to mean that our words and deeds should be so visible that it's like wearing a necklace around our neck that others can see. Wow! Think about it for a minute. When someone thinks of us, do they automatically remember our lives reflect kindness and truth?

Solomon also said to *"write them* [kindness and truth] *upon your heart."* How do we do that? By making those two virtues such a part of our lives that the first reaction to every circumstance is not anger and deception, but kindness and truth.

If we are going to be people of integrity, we must speak the truth even when it might cause a crack in a relationship.

> Honesty is marked as being free from deceit or untruthfulness, being sincere. The Christian life should be one marked with integrity and honesty, yet because we all sin and find it easy to do so, honesty is something we must work hard at! An honest life is important on so many levels from relationships with spouses and children, at our workplace, and interacting with our neighbors. Matthew 7:16 tells us that we are known by our fruit. Let us be

examples of a God of truth and life by living lives of integrity and truthfulness.[11]

6. *Great leaders live by the Marine Corps Code: Semper Fidelis—Always Loyal/Faithful.*

The New World Dictionary of American English defines a loyal person as one who is faithful to those persons, ideals, etc. that one is under obligation to defend, support, or be loyal to. It also defines loyalty as the quality, state, or instance of being loyal; faithfulness or faithful adherence to a person, government, cause, duty, and so on and so forth.[12]

After years of working with leaders around the globe, I can say without contradiction that there are always two groups within an organization. Within those two groups are differing attitudes when it comes to loyalty.

The first group involves those in leadership or in subordinate roles who value integrity and loyalty as the bedrock of the organization. They know that without loyalty, the organization is doomed to failure. They conduct themselves according to the Marine Corps code of *Semper Fidelis*, a Latin phrase meaning *always faithful* or *always loyal*.

The second group shares a different mindset. Their loyalty only extends to the boundaries of a job description. It is the "I will be loyal as long as I get something out of this relationship" attitude. And as soon as they realize there is nothing more you can do to advance their career, color them gone!

On a side note, we must be careful when we discuss loyalty that we don't confuse genuine loyalty based on integrity with "blind loyalty" based on deception. Turning a "blind eye" to illegal acts, abusing others by manipulation, and outright control over people is to be avoided at all costs. The pages of history are littered with evil men who demanded blind loyalty of their followers—Hitler, Stalin, and Osama bin Laden to name a few.

Loyalty is not a one-way street where everything flows from the bottom up. General George Patton put his finger on the issue when he said, "There is a great deal of talk about loyalty from the bottom to the top. Loyalty from the top down is even more necessary and much less prevalent. One of the most frequently noted characteristics of great men who have remained great is loyalty to their subordinates.[13]

If we ever hope to reach our full potential, we must have loyalty. That is the foundation of all we do—in our families, friendships, and business endeavors.

7. Great leaders choose devotion to God over short-term pleasure.

Author Todd Duncan said that integrity is "an unimpaired commitment to personal, moral, and absolute standards."[14] If Duncan's definition is the standard, and I believe it is, I find no better example of that than a man by the name of Joseph. This Old Testament hero had many opportunities to break under pressure, but he refused. You can read the full account of his trials and triumphs in Genesis 37-40.

If you want to see what a profile in integrity looks like, consider some of the trials Joseph endured. God gave him a dream, and that dream initiated unexpected responses:

- His family hated him.
- He was thrown into a pit.
- He was sold into slavery.
- He was falsely accused of sexual assault by his boss's wife.

- He was sent to prison.

Throughout his life, Joseph's integrity was challenged. Whether it was from his family or those who employed him. Even when he was tossed in prison, he didn't allow anger and bitterness to rule his heart—and God honored him for his integrity.

The end of his struggles finds him serving as the number-two man in the administration of the most powerful nation on earth. He was there because each step he took along the journey, he made his devotion to God and his integrity the most important thing in his life. Joseph demonstrated an important principle—your integrity is who you are when no one is looking!

Pastor Bill Purvis writes:

> Strong character is a non-negotiable requirement for achieving our goals and dreams. It is the battering ram that allows us to break through obstacles and grow into a better life. Every challenge we face on the journey to a better life has the potential to either take us down or make us stronger. There's no middle ground. When we face problems and hard times, it's the strength of our character that enables us not only to face the storm, but to turn it to our advantage.[15]

A Final Thought

The end of Joseph's journey looked a lot better than the beginning. His final display of devotion and character came shining through when his family came seeking help. They didn't recognize him at first, and he could have rejected their request, but he didn't.

After his brothers discovered who Joseph was, they were afraid of retribution for their shameful treatment of him. But Genesis 50:20 records Joseph's response: *"You intended to harm me, but God intended it for good to accomplish what is now being done, the saving of many lives."* That is what a man of integrity looks like!

Great Leaders Know How to Wisely Avoid Toxic Relationships

Do not make friends with a hot-tempered person, do not associate with one easily angered, or you may learn their ways and get yourself ensnared.

—Proverbs 22:24-25

Walk away from people who put you down. Walk away from fights that will never be resolved. Walk away from trying to please people who never see your worth. The more you walk away from things that poison your soul, the healthier you will be.

—Unknown Author

Introduction

Most, if not all, leaders understand the importance of building and maintaining positive relationships. Developing relationships among those who are in your charge is an integral component of leadership success. Unfortunately, more than one successful leader has witnessed their influence diminished or even destroyed, because they refused to deal with a toxic relationship.

What is a toxic relationship and why should great leaders avoid them like the plague? The phrase "toxic relationship" generally conveys the idea of a relationship that is very bad, unpleasant, or harmful. According to Asa Don Brown, PhD, "A toxic relationship is any relationship that is unfavorable to you or others."[1]

The writer of Proverbs weighs in on the subject and tells us, *"Walk with the wise and become wise, for a companion of fools suffers harm"* (Proverbs 13:20). I wonder, when Solomon wrote those words, did he have toxic relationships in mind? I think he did.

It has been proven time and again that being in right relationships will help you reach your maximum potential. That is why Solomon's advice is so critical—*it does matter* with whom you associate and who influences your life. Solomon made it clear that if we want to increase our wisdom quotient, it is best to hang around *wise men,* not *wise guys!*

In my travels and responsibilities in World Wide Dream Builders (WWDB), I work with leaders from all walks of life. I have noticed something very critical—hanging around positive, faith-filled people increases my vision and productivity. But when I encounter negative people, I find myself in danger of being influenced by their doubt, fear, confusion, and criticism. As one leadership teacher said, "I can predict your future by looking at your friends. Where they are, is where you're headed."

Your relationships are predictors of your future. If you desire to soar with the eagles, it is necessary to rid yourself of toxic relationships. Allowing toxic relationships keeps you imprisoned with the rest of the chickens in the barnyard of defeat, depression, and disappointment!

In the same article previously quoted, Dr. Asa Brown added:

> The foundations of any relationship, healthy or not, are most commonly established upon mutual admiration and respect, but can, in time, become remarkably unhealthy. It is the poisonous atmosphere that distinguishes a merely bad or troublesome relationship from a toxic relationship. Toxic relationships can prevent those involved from living a productive and healthy life.[2]

Before we look at ways to identify toxic relationships, let's ask a question: Is there a difference between a "bad" relationship and a "toxic" relationship? The answer is yes.

Let's be honest; all relationships have their moments when it seems like nothing you do or say can make things better. But, having a momentary setback in a relationship does not necessarily mean that it is a destructive relationship.

A wise leader understands that you are not going to get along with everyone all of the time. There will be good times, bad times, and all in between. There will be sunny days, cloudy days, and stormy days. But in the final analysis leaders find a way through the fog of difficult relationships.

The bottom line—as long as both parties demonstrate a willingness to work through the difficulties, then the relationship is worth saving. You don't throw away a relationship simply because you had a disagreement, or your feelings were hurt. If that were the case, none of us would ever speak to anyone again!

Carolyn Steber correctly points out the difference between a bad relationship and a toxic relationship:

> In toxic relationships, one or both partners are more likely to be unwilling to change, and there will probably be unhealthy dynamics that won't go away, as a result. But if a relationship simply needs work, both partners will be down to make the effort, and changes will occur. They'll be aware of what's wrong, and will figure out ways to fix it. And they will do so in a kind, understanding, and patient way.[3]

Six Toxic Relationship Warning Signs

1. *You will be drained dry.*

Toxic people always find a way to "take" as they please and never "give" anything in return. Before you realize what is going on, they will drain the life right out of you. A relationship should be two-sided and have positive benefits for both people. If every time you head to the office and the feeling of dread sweeps over you because you know Mr. or Ms. Drain-O will be there, it's time to rethink the direction of the relationship. A relationship that causes an empty feeling in your stomach is not one to celebrate.

Staying in a draining relationship is like handing Dracula the keys to the local blood bank—he may not drink all the blood at once, but given enough time, he will drain it dry! If you find yourself having your energy, vision, and hope sucked out of you, then you need to *run,* not walk away from this person.

2. *You will be sucker punched.*

You know what a sucker punch is, right? It is when someone hits or punches you without warning; and usually when the intended target is not paying attention. In a toxic relationship, the idea of a sucker punch is to catch you off guard and keep you off-balance.

A sucker punch usually comes in the form of a "loaded question," not a clenched fist. Loaded questions are like booby traps set to go off at the most unsuspecting moment. Someone said a loaded question is like a loaded gun with a hair trigger—so be careful how you handle them!

A few samples of loaded questions leaders are asked:

- Do you NOT have a vision for our company/ministry?
- Have you ALWAYS been this insecure?
- WHY have you stopped researching the issue we're facing?
- WILL you admit to the real reason I haven't been promoted?

We must stay focused and refuse to allow this type of person from infecting the entire organization. Being on the receiving end of a sucker punch can be devastating. Sometimes, it's the one you didn't see coming that causes the most damage!

3. *You will be surrounded by negative energy.*

Negative people are to be avoided at all cost. Their attitude and speech are "nothing I do or say is ever good enough." They play the blame game and are always looking for excuses or someone to blame for their situation. They carry their negativity around as a trophy won at the county fair.

The warning is clear: If you surround yourself with negative people, you will end up, in most cases, being just as negative as they are.

Len Sweet wrote:

What is true in nature is true of human nature: 95 percent of the seed you plant is good, while 5 percent is bad. You can trust 95 percent of the people; the other 5 percent of the people are crooks, cranks, cheaters, and crackpots. Do you live your life ruled by the 95 percent or the 5 percent?[4]

Cut the cord by refusing access to negative people, and you will limit what you see and hear. God has appointed certain people to come into your life to help you reach your destiny, but they can be crowded out by a negative atmosphere. The pursuit of success is difficult enough, especially when allowing the wrong people to have a seat at your table.

4. You will be the target of constant accusations.

I have never met anyone who didn't do anything wrong, make a bad decision, or have a failure. We are human, and that's just called life. Taking an action that some would call "a dumb move" is not uncommon, but rather part of the human experience. Bad things happen, so move on. But, not in a toxic relationship, where the relationship is based on you never being right no matter what you do.

As a Christian leader, I have learned that I have an enemy dedicated to my destruction. In Ephesians 6:10-12, the apostle Paul spoke about my enemy, and how I should respond:

Finally, be strong in the Lord and in his mighty power. Put on the full armor of God, so that you can take your stand against the devil's schemes. For our struggle is not against flesh and blood, but against the rulers, against the authorities, against the powers of this dark world and against the spiritual forces of evil in the heavenly realms.

In another Scripture, we are told the devil is the *"accuser of our brothers and sisters"* (Revelation 12:7-12). Even though my enemy is spiritual, he will use other people to carry out his insidious deeds. The goal is to keep me off guard and under the control of toxic people. If you are continually being accused or told that you can't do anything right, look out, there is an enemy afoot, and it's time to take a stand!

5. *You will be bound in chains by emotional control.*

One of the surest signs of a toxic relationship is the use of emotional control. Those of us in leadership have to be especially careful *not* to use any form of emotional bondage to keep followers in line or to accomplish specific tasks.

I have witnessed firsthand how some Christian leaders and business leaders have manipulated their followers to do things by using some form of emotional control.

It usually starts with a simple plea: "If you love me, you will give to my ministry." If that doesn't work, it progresses to pulling out the God-card: "God told me that you must give or He [God] will not be pleased." And on and on it goes until one of two things happen: You will finally decide enough is enough and leave; or, you submit under the weight of emotional bondage.

You can recognize that you are the target of emotional control and should break the chains when you:

- Say "no" and are made to feel guilty.
- Are given the "silent treatment" for offering an opposite opinion.
- Dread being in that person's presence, always.

- Feel rejected because you failed to respond quickly enough.

Author Debbie McDaniel identified this type of person as a "controller."

> This person is a master manipulator and constant controller. They want to be in charge, not just of their lives, but of yours and everyone else's too. They watch you like a hawk, ready to pounce on your every flaw. They micromanage down to the last detail. They have trouble letting go, so they don't, they hold on, too tightly, until it about chokes out all those around them, suffocating others with their drive to be superior.[5]

If you are still not sure if you are in a toxic relationship, ask yourself:

- Do I feel drained every time I am around this person?
- When I leave their presence, do I feel defeated and worthless?
- Am I always made to feel I am wrong, no matter what I do?
- Do I sense the chains of emotional bondage wrapping around me?

6. You will be betrayed.

Human history has given us many names that qualify as the ultimate toxic relationship. But, there is one that stands above the rest. His name was Judas and has been forever connected with the betrayal of the Son of God. (Read Matthew 26 for the full story.) He had every advantage, and yet, in the end, his true nature was revealed by his actions. Judas is the poster boy of toxic relationships.

Consider that Judas:

- Was a part of the core team
- Heard every sermon Jesus gave
- Witnessed many miracles
- Was trusted to keep the money bag

The question remains, why did Judas's relationship with Jesus turn toxic? If he was not happy being a team member, why didn't he leave without doing what he did? After reading and studying the biblical account, I am convinced that Judas felt that he knew better how to run things and was not satisfied with his position. He wanted to be in charge and money was just a small part of the deal. As soon as his true nature was revealed by Jesus, Judas sold his soul to the devil. Can you imagine selling out for a handful of silver coins (John 13:21-30).

Instead of facing his frustrations, Judas took the route that many have traveled: "If I can't have my way, I will 'burn the ministry down' by betraying the leader!" Thank God it didn't work. Why? Because God had a plan to rescue us!

The actions and attitudes of Judas should serve as a warning for us. Be very careful who you allow to sit at the "team table." All it takes is one toxic person to foster division, strife, and cause the team to lose its fire and focus.

People to Avoid

We have only scratched the surface of a very serious issue. The best way to eliminate toxic relationships from forming is to limit the amount of access you give to people.

Your success is determined by those who have access to your time. When you study the secrets of great leaders, you discover they control who enjoys access to their time, and they determine when and where it will happen. The greatest treasure you can give someone is access into your life. People who do not respect your time will not appreciate your wisdom. If you are not careful, you will let wrong priorities and wrong people consume your time.

The Bible is the best book ever written about avoiding toxic relationships. The Scriptures point out there are certain types of people to avoid at all cost. You notice I said to avoid them, but that doesn't mean we should stop praying for people who may have fallen into sinful habits. Just because we don't want someone's harmful influence to impact our lives does not excuse us from taking measures to ask God to open a pathway of spiritual healing and restoration.

I will remind you of what the apostle Paul says in Second Timothy 3:1-5. Paul lays out a list of toxic people. He says, *"mark this."* That means to be aware of what is going on around you. Don't put your head in the sand and hope and pray that everyone will be as accommodating as you are!

I can almost hear someone say, "Wait a minute, Brother Paul, I thought we were supposed to LOVE everybody!" Yes, that's true in one sense of the word, but, I repeat, that doesn't mean we are to allow anyone and everyone to pour their garbage into our lives.

> *But mark this: There will be terrible times in the last days. People will be lovers of themselves, lovers of money, boastful, proud, abusive, disobedient to their parents, ungrateful, unholy, without love, unforgiving, slanderous, without self-control, brutal, not lovers of the good, treacherous, rash, conceited, lovers of pleasure rather than lovers*

of God—having a form of godliness but denying its power. Have nothing to do with such people (2 Timothy 3:1-5).

I once heard a wise man say: "Love your friends, and love your enemies—but you better learn the difference between the two!" We must be harmless as doves, but also wise as serpents! (See Matthew 10:16.)

My Top Six People to Avoid

1. *A violent person.*

My child, if sinners entice you, turn your back on them! They may say, "Come and join us. Let's hide and kill someone! Just for fun, let's ambush the innocent! Let's swallow them alive, like the grave; let's swallow them whole, like those who go down to the pit of death (Proverbs 1:10-12 NLT).

Violent people mislead their companions, leading them down a harmful path (Proverbs 16:29 NLT).

2. *A wicked person.*

The righteous choose their friends carefully, but the way of the wicked leads them astray (Proverbs 12:26).

Do not set foot on the path of the wicked or walk in the way of evildoers. Avoid it, do not travel on it; turn from it and go on your way. For they cannot rest until they do evil; they are robbed of sleep till they make someone stumble. They eat the bread of wickedness and drink the wine of violence (Proverbs 4:14-17).

3. A gossip.

A perverse person stirs up conflict, and a gossip separates close friends (Proverbs 16:28).

4. A person who steals.

My child, if sinners entice you, turn your back on them! They may say, "Come and join us. Let's hide and kill someone! Just for fun, let's ambush the innocent! Let's swallow them alive, like the grave; let's swallow them whole, like those who go down to the pit of death. Think of the great things we'll get! We'll fill our houses with all the stuff we take. Come, throw in your lot with us; we'll all share the loot." My child, don't go along with them! Stay far away from their paths. They rush to commit evil deeds. They hurry to commit murder. If a bird sees a trap being set, it knows to stay away. But these people set an ambush for themselves; they are trying to get themselves killed. Such is the fate of all who are greedy for money; it robs them of life (Proverbs 1:10-19 NLT).

5. A person who engages in deeds of darkness.

Have nothing to do with the fruitless deeds of darkness, but rather expose them (Ephesians 5:11).

6. A person who lives in adultery.

Wisdom will save you also from the adulterous woman, from the wayward woman with her seductive words, who has left the partner of her youth and ignored the covenant she made before God. Surely her house leads down to death

*and her paths to the spirits of the dead. None who go to her
return or attain the paths of life* (Proverbs 2:16-19).

By now you may be saying, "Pastor Paul, that just about eliminates everyone I'm friends with." EXACTLY!

A Final Thought

As a Christian, I'm bound by my commitment to Christ to carry the Gospel to everyone I can. That often means coming in contact with all kinds of people, just like I used to be. I build those relationships with caution, always remembering my reason for the relationship. It's to pull them up while not allowing them to pull me down. They are not my inner circle because when you allow toxic people into your inner circle, you will invariability become contaminated with all their toxic ways.

Becoming an effective leader is hard work, period. And on top of the hard work required, leaders have to be able to recognize when a relationship is turning toxic. It may involve making hard and painful decisions, but cutting someone loose from our sphere of influence may be required to move to the next level of success. There is an old leadership proverb that states, "Be with people who will celebrate you, and not who will tolerate you."

Pastor Joel Osteen agrees. He said, "Don't try to convince anyone that you're a good person. Quit trying to win someone over who isn't kind but only tolerates you—you don't need their approval. Be kind, be respectful, but you don't have to stay...go where you are celebrated. Keep living forward and trust that the right people are there. You never need to convince anyone to love you."[6]

That's good advice. Heed it!

Great Leaders Understand that Success is Not a Secret, It's a Choice

*Do not merely listen to the word, and so deceive yourselves.
Do what it says.*

—James 1:22

*Try not to become a man of success. Rather become a man
of value.*

—Albert Einstein

Introduction

So far we have discussed a great deal about issues and challenges that
leaders face. In Chapter 4, we examined the importance of vision in
the context of "What does it mean to be successful?" To emphasize
the point, I state my premise again:

> Success is found in a person's knowledge of why he or she
> was put on planet Earth, and a willingness to maximize

the person's potential. You hold the key to your future. What you do with that key is entirely up to you. Each of us has a key called "potential." But if you don't use it to unlock your vision, then it becomes nothing more than a reminder of what could have been. (See Chapter 4.)

In this chapter, I give you more insight about what I consider the most profound thought I have when it comes to an understanding of the meaning of success—*success is not a secret, but a choice to be made.* Once that idea firmly plants itself into your mind, you will not be fooled into thinking that success is some mysterious concept or secret that only a few of the "chosen ones" understand.

I cannot count the number of conferences I have attended where the speaker talked about the "secret to success." You can walk into any bookstore or peruse Amazon and other online booksellers and see scores of books on how to achieve leadership success.

I have to confess that deep down in my heart, I don't believe there is a "secret" to success. I am more convinced than ever the reason people are not moving into their destiny and maximizing their potential is not from a lack of knowledge, but from not doing something with the knowledge they have!

The Secret of Success Is Not a Secret

If you want something you have never had, you have to be willing to do something you have never done. To those who say that life is too hard and that's the reason they have given up on their purpose in life, I say "Too hard compared to what?" None of us are exempt from problems. I believe your assignment in life is more significant than any challenges you face.

Your assignment is greater than:

- Your age, young or old
- Past failures
- Opposition to your plans and dreams
- Your current season of life

Challenges are like noses—we all have them! Are you allowing your struggles to stop you dead in your tracks? Or do you see the roadblocks to your destiny as a motivational tool to maximize your God-given abilities to reach your destination? Once again, *it all comes down to the choices you make.*

The responsibility falls on you to know your assignment and discover why God put you on the earth. Once you figure out *why* you are here, then you will understand there is no secret to succeeding in life. Most of life's unhappiness comes from an unwillingness to face the reality that success is a choice, not a secret. If you are not willing to face *that* reality—success is a choice—then you will always be wandering around in the desert of discontentment.

Four Power Thoughts to Change Your View of Success

1. *You can't correct what you don't confront.*

If you are not willing to confront that success is not a secret but a choice, you cannot correct it. Every successful person I know, whether it be in their business, marriage or ministry, have faced challenges that you and I face today. The difference is those who are successful refuse to allow their challenges to defeat them.

I see two groups all the time—the dreamers and the doers.

- *Dreamers.* You know the ones, right? They end up living in a dream world only to discover that dreams are like soap bubbles—one wrong move, and pop they're gone. They talk a lot but accomplish very little. They wonder why others are more successful than they are, yet never bother to investigate to find out why.

- *Doers.* They are the overcomers. You can always tell the overcomers because they talk less and do more. They are willing to face reality and take daily actions to turn their dreams into more than soap bubbles! The doers don't gripe about what life has handed them because they realize that some things in life cannot be controlled. The only thing that they can control are their choices.

The difference between Dreamers and Doers:

- Doers read every day; Dreamers spend too much quality time watching TV and engaging in social media.

- Doers love to compliment; Dreamers love to criticize.

- Doers embrace change; Dreamers reject change.

- Doers talk about new concepts and ideas; Dreamers talk about other people.

- Doers are lifelong learners; Dreamers don't bother, they know it all.

- Doers don't hide from failures; Dreamers find someone to blame.

Which side of this ledger are you on? It's time to choose to turn your dreams into action. It is time for you to find out the *why,* so that you can move forward to the *what!*

2. *You have to close the gap.*

If there is a gap between where you are and where you want to be, do something about it. Life is full of contradictions—between what is going around you and what you know to be true in your heart.

I realize there are some things in life you can't control. You had no say in who your parents were or where you were born. You were not asked how tall you wanted to be or the color of your skin. Those things were left up to your Creator, not you. But you *can* control your choices, and how you react to the contradictions of life.

You see, it's not about what happens *to* you, but what happens *in* you that matters. It's all about your attitude when life hands you a raw deal. Don't wait until there are no problems and everything in your life is perfect before moving forward with your assignment. Why? Because no one is ever going to gain perfection on this side of eternity. Failure to take action with your God-given assignment means that others will never hear your ideas or see your talents. That kind of attitude will set you up for a life of frustration and disappointment.

Many years ago, the Lord taught me a valuable lesson. Our real character is never revealed in our successes but in our failures. When we are put in the pressure cooker of life, we find out what we are on the inside. And, trust me, when the heat is on, our character, whatever is in there, will come bubbling up to the surface.

If you don't reconcile the gap between where you are and where you want to be, you will end up going around in circles. Without knowledge of your assigned purpose, life will become an endless string of activities with little or no significance. Sadly, for many people, life is like riding a rocking horse—lots of motion but no progress. And, the view never changes! If you are sick and tired of being sick and tired, choose to do something about it.

Author and motivational speaker Jim Rohn said, "Every life form seems to strive to its maximum except human beings. How tall will a tree grow? As tall as it possibly can. Human beings on the other hand, have been given the dignity of choice. You can choose to be less. Why not stretch up to the full measure of the challenge and see what all you can do?"[1]

Looping around and repeating the same mistakes day after day and year after year makes life dull and just plain miserable. Why do people keep circling the same issues like a dog chasing his tail?

I see at least two reasons:

1. *Some people hold the belief that everyone else needs to change—not them.* It is the attitude: "I'm perfect, the other folks need to change. The problems I'm having is someone else's fault, not mine." If you ever hope to stop looping around the same issues, you have to recognize that no one is perfect. My friend, we all need to make changes, and that includes you.

2. *Some people hold the belief that success in life is about gathering more information.* And, for that reason, they are always seeking more and better knowledge to find the secret to success. It's like chasing rainbows of information, never realizing that *knowing what to do* and *doing it* are two entirely different things.

In my travels over the past three-plus decades, I have had a constant theme in my messages to pastors and business leaders alike:

Don't just *hear* the Word, *do* the Word. I have spent the better part of my life trying to motivate people to move from *knowing* to *doing*.

In the book of James, he emphasized the necessity of being doers of the Word and not hearers only.

> But **be doers of the word, and not hearers only**, *deceiving yourselves. For if anyone is a hearer of the word and not a doer, he is like a man observing his natural face in a mirror; for he observes himself, goes away, and immediately forgets what kind of man he was. But he who looks into the perfect law of liberty and continues in it, and is not a forgetful hearer but a doer of the work, this one will be blessed in what he does* (James 1:22-25 NKJV).

James uses an interesting phrase, *"not hearers only."* The meaning of the phrase is one of an *auditor*.

* Auditors sit in a classroom to "audit" the class without the normal responsibilities of a regular, matriculating student.
* Auditors take no tests and complete no assignments.
* Auditors are there to only gain information without the burden of doing anything about what they hear.
* Auditors receive no credit for taking the class.

James issues a warning—don't become enamored and excited about gathering information only for the thrill of gaining knowledge. And then refuse to *do* anything with the information you have obtained!

Oliver Wendell Holmes said, "People can be divided into two classes: Those who move ahead and do something, and those who sit still and ask questions and do nothing."[2] I think Holmes perfectly describes most people in life. There are those who move ahead and don't make excuses, while others gather information and do nothing.

3. Turn your belief into action.

A person who *does something* is a person who does not waste time trying to establish belief. Usually we try to develop a belief or faith in something before we take action. People ask me all the time, "Brother Paul, how do I create faith?" Or, "How can I move forward in my faith?" Faith-filled people don't squander their time, emotion, or energy wondering, *Do I really believe this?* They *hear* something, and by faith they *do* something about what they heard.

I am convinced that positive thinkers recognize both sides of any situation. They are not afraid to look at the negative, but choose to spend most of their time and energy on the side that will promote the most favorable outcome. These folks are known as optimistic in their view of life. The term *optimist* comes from the Latin word *optimum* meaning "best." An optimistic person is always expecting the best outcome for any situation.

I am not just talking about the power of positive thinking, but the power of positive living. Positive *thinking* moves me in the right direction, and positive *living* helps me create an atmosphere that others want to be part of. I love what Helen Keller said, *"Optimism is the faith that leads to achievement; nothing can be done without hope."*[3]

I say again, a person who does something is a person who does not waste time trying to establish belief. Belief in what? A belief in what you hear. The Scripture says, *"Consequently, faith comes from hearing the message, and the message is heard through the word about Christ"* (Romans 10:17).

When I was a young man, my father took me out to the backyard and taught me how to use a hammer to drive nails into a wooden door. He looked at me and said, "Paul, this is a hammer, and here are things that a hammer can do." When I used the hammer for the first time, I didn't have to "believe" in it. Why? Because I believed the word my father gave me. I picked up the hammer and drove a nail into a door. It worked the very first time I used it! And it did exactly what my father said it would do. That's how I put my faith in action. I moved in faith on the word I heard from my father.

I have a question for you. Do you have to see results first in order to believe, or do you believe first to see results? Anyone can believe after they see; but successful people hear and believe, and then see the results. Jesus told "Doubting" Thomas, *"Because you have seen me, you have believed; blessed are those who have not seen and yet have believed"* (John 20:29).

Who are you hearing? Do you have a mentor who is willing to help you become successful? You need someone who will point out the landmines, ditches, and potholes on your road to success. If you are smart, you will listen to someone who has already "been there and done that," who can help you avoid unnecessary mistakes. A wise mentor will show you the difference between being busy and being productive—working smarter, not harder.

Are you gathering information from as many sources as you can and still trying to decide if you believe it or not? Or are you acting by faith on what has already been imputed into your heart? My friend, only you can answer the question. Remember, you can't correct what you are unwilling to confront. Maybe it's time to look in the mirror and get honest about changing what is not working.

4. Stop "trying" to be successful.

Most people spend their hours and days *trying* to be successful. Every time I say the word *trying"* it tires me out. People use *trying* as an excuse for why things are not working out; it sounds hollow and insincere. It usually goes like this: I'm *trying* to move forward; I'm *trying* to work things out with my spouse; I'm *trying* to find my purpose; I'm *trying* to build my business; I'm *trying* to grow my ministry; on and on, *ad nauseam*.

Trying is a victim's mentality. I don't feel sorry for someone who is just trying. Don't misunderstand, I have compassion and love for people and will do everything in my power to see people succeed. But, my dear friend, if you are just trying, you are never going to get to where you want to go.

Let's say somebody owes you $1,000. He comes to you one day and says, "You know I'm going to TRY to pay you back." What the person is really saying to you is, "I would not count on ever seeing your money again." How would that make you feel? Not very hopeful, I'm sure.

The opposite of trying is commitment. The word *commitment* means an agreement or pledge to do something in the future; the state or an instance of being obligated or emotionally impelled.

What you would like to hear from someone who owes you money is, "I'm not going to TRY to pay you back, I'm COMMITTED to paying you back." Making a commitment moves you from *trying*, to getting it done no matter what!

I see so many people who are ruled by their emotions. One day they are on the mountaintop, and the next day they are lower than low. If you are being governed by how you feel daily, you have set yourself up for failure. I don't know how many times I had to set my emotions aside and follow through with a commitment I made.

I attended a Celebration of Life for a pastor's wife who had passed away. The pastor said something at the end of the service that made an impact on me: *"No sermon ever preached, no matter how eloquent it was presented, can rival a life well lived!"* No truer words were ever spoken. Sermons are about words, and life is about making the right choices and taking action. You *cannot* build a life worth living based on words alone. Period!

- Commitment moves you toward the success you are seeking.

- Commitment is revealed by what you have produced or failed to produce, up to now.

- Commitment and faithfulness are two sides of the same coin.

- Commitment is a function—not just a word without purpose—that alters your behavior.

Your failure to commit results in you being committed to failure!

—Tsika

Consider these truths about a lack of commitment:

- When I am unclear about my commitment, I procrastinate. When I am clear about my commitment, I take action.

- When I am unclear about my commitment, I talk about my dream. When I am clear about my commitment, I build my dream.

- When I am unclear about my commitment, I maintain my image. When I am clear about my commitment, I maintain my integrity.

- When I am unclear about my commitment, I play it safe. When I am clear about my commitment, I will do whatever is necessary to succeed.

- When I am unclear about my commitment I am lazy, dull, and confused. When I am clear about my commitment, I am energized, empowered, and intentional with my follow-through based on the information I have.

Are you clear or unclear about your commitment? Has your behavior been altered by the commitments you have made? Has your commitment altered where you go, the people you talk to, and what you read? If your lifestyle has not been altered to conform to your purpose in life, then I have to question your commitment. A genuine commitment is a function that *will* alter your behavior. No behavior altered means no genuine commitment.

Years ago, I committed to add value, wisdom, and empowerment to as many leaders as possible. It would be fair to say that my commitment has altered my life. As of this writing, I am at the age when most people have already retired. Instead of retiring, I fly hundreds of thousands of air miles every year to speak and minister to leaders. Instead of laying around all day, I get up before dawn and spend time writing books and messages that will make a difference in people's lives. I watch what I eat and exercise daily. I do everything possible to maintain my health. Why do I do these things? I value my commitment more than temporary pleasure.

My friend, when you know your purpose and are willing to do everything humanly possible to succeed, you don't have time to sit around and hope things work out. You can't be lazy and expect to accomplish your assignment. Proverbs 10:4 says, *"Lazy hands make for poverty, but diligent hands bring wealth."*

> Great leaders are focused but not obsessed, disciplined but not legalistic. Great leaders are dedicated without becoming unhinged zealots. The bottom line is balance in leadership as it is in life.
> —Dr. Mark Rutland

Years ago, I ran across the following statement by Tim Ferris: "The measure of a person's success in life can normally be reduced to the number of uncomfortable conversations they are willing to have." What a powerful truth! When is the last time you had a conversation that made you really uncomfortable? With your spouse? With your mentor? With your pastor? With your children? With a friend? With yourself? I believe with all my heart the reason people don't succeed in life is an unwillingness to have uncomfortable conversations.

I look at people who are successful in all types of endeavors. Some have built businesses, while others have seen success in establishing great ministries. They are the go-getters, achievers, and the risk-takers. I ask myself, *What makes them so successful? What makes them so different? Are they in a separate category from the rest of us?* I don't think so. They are ordinary people who have made extraordinary choices with the knowledge they have. They were willing to have uncomfortable conversations and look at the person in the mirror. They stopped looking for more information and starting doing what they knew to do.

We are selling our future on the auction block of *Someday,* instead of purchasing our future in the marketplace of daily commitments.

> Someday is no day; because you made that promise yester-day; and tomorrow will be the same; and there's no one left to blame.
>
> —TSIKA

A Final Thought

I hope I've made it clear there is no secret to success. Are you ready to stop the merry-go-round and do something about your assignment? Why not start taking action today? Set your sails to catch the winds of excitement that come when you commit to your God-given assignment.

3-D Bottom Line to Success

Let me offer you my 3-D Bottom Line to Success:

1. *Define what you want to accomplish.* Be specific. (If you can't define what you want to achieve in life, don't go any further until you do.)

2. *Develop the necessary steps to get there.* Determine the price you are going to have to pay. (When you know the direction you want to go, plan a strategy to get there.)

3. *Do the required actions necessary.* (Put the first two steps into action!)

> A warrior is an average person with laser-like focus. Focus requires an active, conscious commitment. Over and over, daily ask yourself: Am I doing what's necessary to accomplish my dreams?
>
> —BRUCE LEE

You and I have an enemy that will do anything and everything to rob us of our dreams. If we allow him to break our focus from our God-given assignment, we will never see all that God intended for our lives.

Life is not about winning or losing or success or failure, but learners and non-learners. Life is about being a lifelong learner—learning from our mistakes and taking action to correct them. Not one single person has ever become successful without making mistakes. What sets those who are successful apart is their willingness to do something that many people refuse to do—learn from and correct whatever went wrong. You see, their commitments altered their behavior, and they made the necessary course corrections to fulfill their purpose!

Let me ask you again:

If not...why not?

If not you...who?

If not here...where?

If not now...when?

If you are not living your dreams and walking in your destiny, there is no one to blame but you. The good news is you can do something about it starting today, right now.

I encourage you to *take action that will change your life for the best!*

As I was putting the finishing touches on this chapter, I was reminded of something that happened to me recently. I was at our Bay House finishing some writing and was planning to head back to my office, some twenty minutes away. After I locked up, I stopped to look inside one more time to make sure everything was secure. As I looked through the window, the sun reflected my image in the glass.

I stopped dead in my tracks. I didn't leave—I walked back inside and sat down wrote the following poem:

The Man in the Window

I walked by a window the other day
and looked inside to see.
But all I saw was an older man
who looked very similar to me.
I smiled then I laughed when I looked again;
and wondered how I got there.
I'd like to go back and start over again
and this time really show I care.
I'd care about those put in my life;
I'd care about family and friends;
I'd care about those who need real help;
I'd care and I'd help them to mend.
If you ask me today do I have regrets,
I'd have to say with grief,
That man I saw has many;
But today I have belief...
That Christ is here to help me be
The man I should have been;
And when I pass that window,
I'll never see that man again.
—PAUL TSIKA, May 11, 2019

That man in the window—me—determined to pay any price and go to any lengths to fulfill my destiny.

How about you?

Are you ready?

GREAT LEADERS HAVE A LEGACY WORTH FOLLOWING

A good person leaves an inheritance for their children's children, but a sinner's wealth is stored up for the righteous.

—PROVERBS 13:22

All good men and women must take responsibility to create legacies that will take the next generation to a level we could only imagine.

—JIM ROHN[1]

Introduction

In my book *Sequoia-Size Success,* I wrote, *"Success without a successor is tantamount to failure."* I don't have any empirical evidence to back up that statement, but it does bring the reality of leaving a legacy into focus. The issue is not if we choose to leave a legacy for the next generation to follow—but what kind of legacy we are going to leave. Whether we plan for it or not, we all leave something behind.

Here's a sobering thought: Whether we want to admit it or not, or even talk about it, we are all going to die someday—no exceptions. Period. As one old sage said, "Nobody gets off this planet alive!" (Well, maybe astronauts, but that is only temporary.) We may not be able to take it with us, but we will surely leave it behind—our legacy.

I will admit there are more exciting subjects to discuss than our mortality. But as each birthday comes and goes, I am reminded that one day I too will step across the Jordan, and make the trip into eternity. Each turn of the calendar forces me to think about what I will leave behind for the generations who come after me.

The following story is a stark reminder that everything we do has a powerful effect on many lives, on many levels:

> One day in 1888, a wealthy and successful man was reading what was supposed to be his brother's obituary in a French newspaper. As he read, he realized that the editor had confused the two brothers and had written an obituary for *him* instead. The headline proclaimed, "The merchant of death is dead," and then described a man who had gained his wealth by helping people to kill one another. Not surprisingly, he was deeply troubled by this glimpse of what his legacy might have been had he actually died on that day. It is believed that this incident was pivotal in motivating him to leave nearly his entire fortune following his actual death eight years later to fund awards each year to give to those whose work most benefitted humanity. This is, of course, the true story of Alfred Nobel, the inventor of dynamite and the founder of the Nobel Prize.[2]

The transformation of Alfred Nobel is a reminder of how important it is to find the true meaning and value in our lives, especially in light of eternity. I doubt anyone who reads this book will have the opportunity to read about their death before they die. But Mr. Nobel did, and it changed him and the world forever!

The typical attitude among today's youth is, "I have all the time in the world to achieve my goals, and live out my dreams. I can live my life as I please." But in light of eternity, our life is but a brief moment in time, and what we do in those fleeting moments determines our destiny and our legacy. Benjamin Franklin famously said, "If you would not be forgotten as soon as you are dead, either write something worth reading or do something worth writing."[3]

In the book of James, we are told not to take our life for granted:

Now listen, you who say, "Today or tomorrow we will go to this or that city, spend a year there, carry on business and make money." Why, you do not even know what will happen tomorrow. What is your life? You are a mist that appears for a little while and then vanishes (James 4:13-14).

What does legacy mean?

Merriam-Webster defines *legacy* as "something transmitted by or received from an ancestor or predecessor or from the past."[4] Our legacy is what people will be saying about our contribution to planet Earth after we are gone. Legacy is what people remember about us after the crying stops.

Carve your name on hearts, not tombstones. A legacy is etched into the minds of others and the stories they share about you.

—SHANNON L. ALDER[5]

Four Keys to Building a Lasting Legacy

Key 1: Develop a Plan

At some level, most, if not all of us, desire to leave something far greater than what *WE* inherited from prior generations. If that desire is not turned into action, then it will be left up to others to decide whether our contribution was positive or negative.

Do you have a strategy? According to *businessdictionary.com,* the word *strategy* denotes two essential factors:

1. A *method or plan* chosen to bring about a desired future, such as achievement of a goal or solution to a problem.

2. The art and science of *planning and marshaling* resources for their most efficient and effective use. The term is derived from the Greek word for generalship or leading an army.[6]

Nothing is ever accomplished without a strategy, a plan to get us where we want to go. We take great pains to plan all sorts of things:

- Our careers
- Who we are going to marry
- Where we want to live
- How many children we will have
- Where we spend our vacations
- What kind of car we drive
- Even our funeral arrangements

Why not become intentional about our legacy?

The desire to leave a legacy may be the height of altruism, for it is a gift to the future; you may never witness the benefits of it nor feel the appreciation of others. Creating your legacy does not happen overnight, and it doesn't come without a strategy and hard work.[7]

Nothing is ever built without a strategic plan. Someone who had a dream strategically planned every magnificent structure you see. The architect took a vision and turned it into reality because of one thing: a well-thought-out and well-executed plan!

1. A plan is your road map revealing where you are and where you want to go.

2. A plan creates a single-minded focus to keep you on course.

3. A plan gives you incentive to "keep at it" when things get tough.

4. A plan, well-developed and executed, will motivate others to follow your lead.

5. A plan gives you a sense of purpose that will help develop your potential.

Key 2: Reproduce Yourself

I am not talking about reproducing yourself biologically, but reproducing yourself by pouring into the generations that come after you. It may be a family member, a protégé, or a coworker. Reproducing yourself is a key to legacy building. I often breakdown the word *passion* into three words in trying to define its essence: PASS-It-ON. What a person is passionate about is what will be passed on to others.

The law of reproduction is the fundamental law of nature and an integral part of God's creative process. Every seed that is planted carries its own unique DNA. If we plant corn, we can expect corn to be the result, not soybeans! Scripture tells us that we reap what we sow (Galatians 6:7). The law of reproduction works both in the natural and in the spiritual.

Wise leaders understand that if they want to reproduce themselves for generations to come, they must sow seeds in good soil. The right seed sown in good soil is necessary to produce a maximum harvest. The steps we take today will become the well-worn path of tomorrow's success.

The apostle Paul believed in the law of reproduction. He had a young protégé named Timothy. In his last letter to him, Paul reminded young Timothy the necessity of passing on the fundamental truths that Timothy had learned from his mentor.

> *You then, my son, be strong in the grace that is in Christ Jesus. And **the things you have heard me say** in the presence of many witnesses **entrust to reliable people** who will also be qualified **to teach others*** (2 Timothy 2:1-2).

But, a word of caution must be expressed when it comes to recognizing those we deem worthy of following in our footsteps. Paul had warned Timothy not to lay hands—the act of recognizing leadership—too quickly on anyone (1 Timothy 5:22).

Why?

J. Oswald Sanders explains the matter in his excellent book *Spiritual Leadership*:

> Paul warns that a person not ready for leadership, and thrust into the role, "may become conceited and fall under

the same judgment as the devil" (1 Timothy 3:6). A new convert does not yet possess the spiritual stability essential to leading people wisely. It is unwise to give key positions too early even to those who demonstrate promising talent, lest status spoils them. The story of the church and its mission is filled with examples of failed leaders who were appointed too soon. A novice suddenly placed in authority over others faces the danger of inflated ego. Instead, the promising convert should be given a widening opportunity to serve at humbler and less prominent tasks that will develop both natural and spiritual gifts. He should not be advanced too fast, least he becomes puffed up. Neither should he be repressed, lest he become discouraged.[8]

There are not many things in life more satisfying than investing seeds of development into someone else. It has been said that *we make a living by what we get, but we make a life by what we give.*

Training and investing in someone else may not take you outside of your current circle. Most of us will never travel to a foreign country to train someone, unless you are called by God to do so; however, we can open the door for a friend who shows potential, help others discover their purpose in life, or simply help people in the community. It may be that we are training someone to take our place. One of the main goals of leadership is to train others who will be capable and equipped to take over.

Laurie Beth Jones, author of *Jesus CEO,* recounted her idea of how Jesus reproduced Himself in His disciples.

I have personally witnessed the downfall of an executive director who had ruled a huge organization for nearly

12 years, largely through smoke and mirrors. When his incompetence finally came collapsing down upon him and he was relieved of his command, there was quite a mess to clean up. The problem was, it wasn't just his incompetence that had to be corrected. He had multiplied himself by hiring people who were far less qualified, and hence less of a threat, to him in every area. This organization had a core of incompetence that, like a cancer, had infiltrated every department and nearly caused the demise of the entire organization.

By contrast, Jesus as CEO was eager and intent upon hiring people He felt could replace Him. "Greater things than I have done shall you do," He promised. Jesus did not hoard or guard the power of His office. He kept teaching and sharing and demonstrating it so team members would learn that they too had the power to do what He had done.

In order for Him to be so generous with His power, Jesus obviously had to have been extremely secure. He repeatedly affirmed and clearly understood His standing with "the chairman of the board." He never doubted that, when it was all over, He would be sitting at the head table. His job was to fill that table and make sure others were sitting with Him. Jesus trained His replacements![9]

Key 3: Don't Drop the Baton

The phrase "pass the baton" refers to a relay race event in track and field. A relay team consisting of four runners who each run a portion, or "leg," of the race. As the runner approaches the exchange zone, he must hand off the baton to the next runner who is standing there with his motor running waiting to turn on the jets. But if the exchange is muffed and the baton is dropped, it's "game over" for the team.

In the 2008 Olympic games held in Beijing, China, the American relay team was poised to take on all comers. Observers of the games projected there would be a winner-take-all race between the Jamaicans and the Americans. The race never happened. The American team never made it past the preliminary heat.

What happened?

Howard Fendrich of the Associated Press recounts the sad ending to what could have been a successful event for the American runners:

> Tyson Gay stuck his left hand behind him, waiting to feel the red baton's cool metal to make contact. Still waiting, Gay looked ahead and began to take off. Now accelerating, he glanced back at Darvis Patton, his U.S. teammate in a 400-meter relay preliminary heat. A moment later, Patton let go of the stick, and Gay squeezed his hand shut—empty.
>
> Gay never did feel that baton Thursday night, never did get to run his anchor leg, never did get to even compete in a final at the Beijing Olympics, much less win a medal, let alone gold. Instead, the stick slammed to the wet track, a not-so-subtle symbol of American favorites' foibles at the Bird's Nest.[10]

The American team failed at the most critical moment—the handoff. It didn't matter if they were the fastest on the track that day; what mattered most was passing the baton, perfectly, at the exact time. Anything less was a failure.

Tony Wang, in the article "Passing the Baton," states the following is needed to qualify for a good pass:

- Both runners must be running so that they do not lose time.
- There must be trust and confidence that the team member will hand it over properly.
- A runner receiving the baton cannot look back or swerve out of his lane.
- It requires knowledge of each other's ability.
- The runner passing the baton has to tell the other runner when to go. If he says, "Go!" too early, he won't have time to catch him and give him the baton.
- It also requires strict obedience to the rules.[11]

Imagine for a moment that leadership is an Olympic sport, and you have entered your "team" in the relay race.

You are kneeling at the starting block—baton firmly in hand. As the gun sounds, you burst out of the blocks and you pay no attention to what's behind you, only keeping your eyes straight ahead—hoping against hope that you make a perfect handoff.

As you near the exchange zone, you are running at full tilt, and you know the race will be won or lost…right here, right now. It all depends on the exchange. You glimpse your teammate who is leaning forward, straining every muscle, waiting to hear the signal, GO, and feel the baton in his hand.

You make a clean handoff and watch as your team member takes the baton and runs with blazing speed to the next exchange. Your part is over, finished. You have completed your leg of the race, and now you can enjoy watching the rest of the team compete for the prize.

Here's what I've learned:

- Timing is everything.
- It matters who is on the team.
- If I pass the baton too early or too late, the next in line will fail.
- The baton is passed when I am at full tilt, not when I am sitting on the sidelines, stretching my muscles.

I will never pass the baton to someone who only "thinks" about joining the team.

Writing for the *Legacy Project*, Susan Bosak made an interesting observation:

> Where do you think it's best to plant a young tree: a clearing in an old-growth forest or an open field? Ecologists tell us that a young tree grows better when it's planted in an area with older trees. The reason, it seems, is that the roots of the young tree are able to follow the pathways created by former trees and implant themselves more deeply. Over time, the roots of many trees may actually graft themselves to one another, creating an intricate, interdependent foundation hidden under the ground. In this way, stronger trees share resources with weaker ones so that the whole forest becomes healthier. That's legacy: an interconnection across time, with a need for those who have come before us and a responsibility to those who come after us.[12]

Key 4: Focus on True Wealth

King Solomon wrote in Proverbs 13:22, *"A good person leaves an inheritance for their children's children, but a sinner's wealth is stored up for the righteous."* You might be thinking that Solomon was referring to *just* material wealth when he wrote about leaving an inheritance for your children's children.

No doubt material wealth is included in Solomon's thinking, but leaving a legacy is more than making sure your final arrangements and finances are in order. Of course all of those things are important, as well as making sure you have a will and the proper legal documents concerning your estate. The last thing any of us would want to do is leave our families in a bind and let the courts decide who gets what we leave behind.

But, there is more to it than that.

Jesus talked more about money than any other subject. That's right; He spent more time warning about the dangers of wealth than teaching on Heaven and hell combined! Why? Jesus knew that when the focus is on the accumulation of money, there is a danger that the love of money can replace our devotion to God.

There is nothing wrong with having things, as long as things don't have us. We will not be judged by the amount of money in our bank account, but rather how we used what we had to bless others.

The apostle Paul admonished Timothy:

> *Command those who are rich in this present world not to be arrogant nor to put their hope in wealth, which is so uncertain, but to **put their hope in God**, who richly provides us with everything for our enjoyment. Command them to **do good**, to **be rich in good deeds**, and to **be generous and***

willing to share. *In this way they will lay up treasure for themselves as a firm foundation for the coming age, so that they may take hold of the life that is truly life* (1 Timothy 6:17-19).

God measures our lives not by how much we possess, but by how much we give! Reverend Billy Graham had it right when he said, "The greatest legacy one can pass on to one's children and grandchildren is not money or other material things accumulated in one's life, but rather a legacy of *character and faith.*"[13]

Graham said the most important aspects of leaving a legacy is NOT money or material things, but two essentials—*character and faith.* Let's consider each personally:

Character: What is character, and how is it different from my reputation?

- Reputation is what others *say* about me.
- Character is what *I am* when no one is watching.
- Reputation is formed by actions that I want *others* to see.
- Character is formed by *my response* to the pressures of life.

Our hope and prayer should be that our reputation and character are unified, so that what we are on the inside is reflected by what we do on the outside!

> The results we achieve in any situation depend, more than anything else, on how we respond to the events and circumstances we are facing. And, it is our character that determines how we will respond to those events and

circumstances. Therefore, it is our character that determines our success.[14]

Faith: How do you leave a legacy of faith?

- *Walk your talk.* Set a "faith" example in front of your children. Don't just tell them the importance of living for the Lord, show them by your actions.

- *Show them your faith when the storms hit.* It's easy to live for the Lord when the sun is shining. But what about those times when life falls apart?

- *Teach them the importance of prayer and reading God's Word, the Bible.* Don't let Sunday be the only time they can see how much your relationship to God and His Word mean to you. Walking out your faith is a daily occurrence.

- Commit to nurturing your family in the things of God. There is nothing more important!

A Final Thought

It doesn't matter whether you are a nurse, pastor, attorney, artist, laborer, business executive, farmer, stay-at-home parent, teacher, etc., all of us, *yes that includes you,* will leave a legacy.

Through the corridors of time, countless men and women, from all walks of life have left this world powerful legacies. They were ordinary people who did extraordinary things.

Just name a few:

- Martin Luther King Jr.
- Mother Teresa
- Albert Einstein

- Rich DeVos
- Steve Jobs
- Henry Ford
- Helen Keller
- Alexander Graham Bell
- Margaret Thatcher
- Ron Puryear
- Billy Graham
- Harriet Beecher Stowe
- Ronald Reagan

And, so many more who have left amazing legacies that perhaps only their family, friends, and or coworkers will remember. Each righteous legacy is valuable to the generations that follow.

But there was and is One who stands above the rest. More than two thousand years ago, He walked among men, as a man. Who was this Man who changed the world and left a legacy that is still being walked out today?

Jesus Christ—the greatest leader who ever lived!

He left a legacy of love and humility. Jesus showed us what a real relationship with God looks like. He demonstrated forgiveness and compassion for everyone, including those who were deemed too far gone to be redeemed. He loved everyone the same. And at the end of His life, He even prayed for those who nailed Him to a cross to die.

As you consider what kind of legacy you want to leave, you will find no better example than Jesus Christ.

To this you were called, because Christ suffered for you, leaving you an example, that you should follow in his steps (1 Peter 2:21).

EPILOGUE

THE MILLION-DOLLAR QUESTION

Through the years, I have been asked all sorts of questions concerning leadership. But at the top of the list is what I call the million-dollar question, which is: "Are leaders born, or made?"

On one side are those who believe that leaders are born with certain traits and abilities that make them natural leaders. They point to historical figures including John F. Kennedy, Martin Luther King Jr., Winston Churchill, Ronald Reagan, and Susan B. Anthony as examples. They highlight the idea that it seems all great leaders have a "natural charisma" that inspires others to follow them. It's as if to say, "If you are not a born leader, you don't have a chance of becoming one."

On the other side are those who believe that, as Warren Bennis observed, "As countless deposed kings and hapless heirs to great fortunes can attest, true leaders are not born, but made, and usually self-made."[1]

I have to agree with Bennis. No matter which side you are on, you will have to admit that the vast majority of great leaders had more than a charming personality and a winning smile. If you do a deep dive into anyone's life you consider a leader, you will find common characteristics that were not encoded into their DNA at birth.

Common traits such as:

- Vision
- Passion
- Integrity
- Trust
- Curiosity and daring[2]

Genuine leadership skills are not acquired overnight. Picking up a *Time-Life* book or buying a subscription to *Success Magazine* will not make you a leader. No more than watching a documentary on Tiger Woods winning the Masters Golf Tournament will give you the knowledge and skill to pick up a set of golf clubs and head to Augusta National.

I have yet to find a leader who can walk out of a weekend seminar on "How to Change the World in 90 Days or Less" and actually change the world! It doesn't work that way. That is not to say that I don't think listening to sound teaching, buying books, or attending seminars are helpful—they are.

Please don't make the mistake of thinking if you can gain a specific title that will make you a leader. Don't let someone convince you that if you have a sign on your door that says, "BOSS" you are the leader of your organization.

- Great leaders value function over titles.
- Great leaders do more than talk a good game—they go down on the field and play.
- Great leaders are willing to put into practice all the knowledge and skill they learn to benefit others.
- Great leaders recognize that it may take years of hard work to realize their God-given potential.

Where do you stand?

Before you put this book down, I encourage you to take a simple test and see where you stand. J. Oswald Sanders, in his book *Spiritual Leadership,* included a chapter titled "Can You Become a Leader?" Sanders chose the greatest leader who ever lived as his model—Jesus.

Sanders emphasized the fact that when Jesus chose His leaders, it was not based on the standards outlined by the prevailing thinking of the day. Jesus was not put off by their lack of skills, education, or social refinement. Jesus saw something in the men He chose that others could not see—*potential.* Jesus knew that with proper training these men of various backgrounds would turn the world upside down.

In *Spiritual Leadership,* Sanders observed: "To their latent talents were added fervent devotion and fierce loyalty, honed in the school of failure and fatigue. If we look carefully, we should be able to detect our leadership potential."[3]

Sanders also shares twenty-seven questions to help you discover your leadership potential:

1. How do you identify and deal with bad habits? To lead others, you must master your appetites.

2. How well do you maintain self-control when things go wrong? A leader must be calm in a crisis and resilient in disappointment.

3. To what degree do you think independently? A leader cannot wait for others to make up his or her mind. But when part of a team, you must be a team player.

4. How well do you handle criticism?

5. Can you turn disappointment into a creative, new opportunity?

6. Do you readily gain the cooperation of others and win their respect and confidence? Genuine leadership doesn't have to manipulate or pressure others.

7. Can you exert discipline without making a power play? True leadership is an internal quality of the spirit and needs no show of external force.

8. In what situations have you been a peacemaker?

9. Do people trust you with difficult and delicate matters?

10. Can you induce people to do happily some legitimate thing that they would not normally wish to do?

11. Can you accept opposition to your viewpoint or decision without taking offense?

12. Can you make and keep friends? Your circle of loyal friends is an index of your leadership potential.

13. Do you depend on the praise of others to keep you going?

14. Are you at ease in the presence of strangers?

15. Are people who report to you generally at ease? A leader should be sympathetic and friendly.

16. Are you interested in people? All types? All races? No prejudice?

17. Are you tactful? Can you anticipate how your words will affect a person?

18. Is your will strong and steady? Leaders cannot vacillate, cannot drift with the wind.

19. Can you forgive? Or do you nurse resentments and harbor ill feelings toward those who have injured you?

20. Are you reasonably optimistic?

21. Have you identified a master passion such as that of Paul, who said, "This *one thing* I do!" Such singleness of motive will focus your energies and powers on the desired objective. Leaders need a strong focus.

22. How do you respond to new responsibility?

How we handle relationships tells a lot about our potential for leadership. R.E. Thompson suggests these tests:

23. Do other people's failures annoy or challenge you?

24. Do you use people, or cultivate people?

25. Do you direct people, or develop people?

26. Do you criticize or encourage?

27. Do other people's success cause you to rejoice or become resentful?[4]

These self-examinations mean little unless we act to correct our deficits and fill in the gaps of our training.[5]

My heart's desire for this book is that it finds its way into your head, heart, and life. Don't live your life only listening to others talk about successful leadership. But take their words and let God convert them into reality in your life. *Because leadership has a language—and that language is YOU!*

ENDNOTES

Chapter 1

1. Deborah Day, *Be Happy Now! Become the Active Director of Your Life* (Bloomington, IL: Xlibris, 2010), 25.

2. Vocabulary.com, Negativity; https://www.vocabulary.com/dictionary/ negativity; accessed January 18, 2018.

3. Terry Orlick, PhD, *In Pursuit of Excellence* (Champaign, IL: Human Kinetics Publishers, 2008), 171.

4. James Allen quote, as cited in *As a Man Thinketh by James Allen— Animated Book Summary* posted on November 02, 2017 by Lohn Leyo; https://www.woolibrary.com/man-thinketh-james-allen -animated-book-summary/; accessed January 18, 2018.

5. Paul Tsika, *Sequoia-Size Success,* Principle Six (Midfield, TX: Plow On Publications, 2005), 77-78.

6. Seinfeld Scripts, "The Pilot"; https://www.seinfeldscripts.com/ ThePilot.html; accessed January 2, 2020.

7. Christie Marie Sheldon, *How Negative Energy Affects Your Life and How to Clear It;* https://blog.mindvalley.com/negative-energy/; accessed January 3, 2020.

8. Mahatma Gandhi quoted in *Tiger Heart, Tiger Mind: How to Empower Your Dream* by Ron Rubin and Stuart Avery Gold (New York: Newmarket Press, 2005), 86.

9. Richie Norton, "How to Succeed (or Fail) at Anything: Wishers, Worriers & Warriors"; http://richienorton.com/2015/05/ beawarrior/; accessed January 10, 2020.

10. Lawrence Robinson, Melinda Smith, Jeanne Segal, "Laughter is the Best Medicine"; *HelpGuide;* https://www.helpguide.org/articles/ mental-health/laughter-is-the-best-medicine.htm; accessed January 2, 2020.

11. P.D. Ouspensky, *The Psychology of Man's Possible Evolution*, Fourth Lecture (1950), 70. https://en.wikiquote.org/wiki/Emotions; accessed January 10, 2020.

12. Archie Manley, "20 Famous People Who Succeeded Against All Odds," http://www.archiemanley.com/20-famous-people-who -succeeded-against-all-odds/; accessed February 9, 2018.

Chapter 2

1. Walter M. Schirra Sr.; https://www.artofmanliness.com/articles/the -ultimate-collection-of-quotes-about-fatherhood/; accessed January 22, 2020.

2. Kent Sanders, "Why I Don't Force My Son to Play Sports," *The Good Men Project,* September 23, 2015; https://goodmenproject .com/ featured-content/why-i-dont-force-my-son-to-play-sports-dg/; accessed January 10, 2020.

3. John Tierney, "The Doofus Dad," *The New York Times,* June 18, 2005; http://www.nytimes.com/2005/06/18/opinion/the-doofus -dad. html; accessed January 3, 2020.

4. Seth Stevenson, "The Reign of the Doltish Dad"; *Slate.com,* March 26, 2012; http://www.slate.com/articles/arts/branded/2012/03/ huggies_diapers_first_its_ad_used_a_doltish_dad_then_came _the_outcry_.html; accessed January 3, 2020.

5. Ibid.

6. Dr. David Popenoe, Professor of Sociology at Rutgers University and Co-Director of the National Marriage Project, quoted in the *Focus on the Family* article, "Fathers and the Influence They Have on Their Sons"; https://www.focusonthefamily.com/family-q-and-a/parenting/ fathers-and-the-influence-they-have-on-their-sons#fn1; accessed January 3, 2020). Quote also from David Popenoe's book *Life Without Father* (New York: The Free Press, 1996).

7. Brett and Kate McKay, *The Importance of Fathers (According to Science),* https://www.artofmanliness.com/2015/06/19/the -importance-of- fathers-according-to-science/; accessed January 3, 2020).

8. Matt Walsh, "3 Things A Father Must Teach His Son So That His Son Doesn't End Up Dead Or In Prison," https://www.dailywire.com/ news/27618/walsh-matt-walsh?utm_source=facebook&ut _medium=social&utm_content=062316-news&utm _campaign=benshapiro; accessed March 11, 2018.

9. Rick Johnson interview for *Relevant Magazine* article, "A Fatherless Generation"; https://relevantmagazine.com/life/whole-life/features/2721-a-fatherless-generation/; accessed January 3, 2020.
10. *The Wussification of America: How We're Creating a Nation of* Wimps, http://thebertshow.com/nationofwimps/; accessed January 3, 2020.
11. Will Leitch, "How to Raise a Boy: I'm not sure what to think about what my dad tried to teach me. So what should I teach my sons?" *The Cut,* March 5, 2018; https://www.thecut.com/2018/03/will-leitch-on-raising-sons-in-2018.html/; accessed January 10, 2020.
12. Clarence Budington Kelland; https://en.wikiquote.org/wiki/Talk:Fathers; accessed January 10, 2020.

Chapter 3

1. James Allen, *As a Man Thinketh* (Om Books International Corporate & Editorial Office A-12, Sector 64, Noida 201 301 Uttar Pradesh, India); Kindle Edition accessed April 3, 2018.
2. Glenn and Diane Davis, *The Importance of Thinking*, https://www.learn-to-read-prince-george.com/about-us.html; accessed April 4, 2018.
3. Fred Rogers, *25 Famous Thinkers and Their Inspiring Daily Rituals,* http://www.onlinecollege.org/2010/01/11/25-famous-thinkers-and-their-inspiring-daily-rituals/; accessed January 10, 2020.
4. Elizabeth Fillppouli, "Successful Leaders & Global Thinkers Forum," October 13, 2012, *huffingtonpost.com;* https://www.huffingtonpost.com/elizabeth-filippouli/successful-leaders-global-thinkers_b_1773958.html; accessed January 10, 2020.
5. Ali Rushdan, "Lessons In Innovation From Six of the World's Most Creative Thinkers"; https://www.fastcompany.com/3040434/lessons-in-innovation-from-some-of-the-worlds-most-creative-thinkers; accessed January 10, 2020.
6. Seneca quote is found in a 1920 translation published of Seneca the Younger's work titled *Epistle LXXI: On The Supreme Good.* Seneca used figurative language from the domains of archery and navigation to make his point about the desirability of specific goals; https://quoteinvestigator.com/2011/11/25/favorable-wind/; accessed April 10, 2018.
7. Henry Ford, as quoted in *The High School Teacher*, Vol. XI (1935), 60; https://en.wikiquote.org/wiki/Henry_Ford; accessed April 10, 2018.

8. Mujtaba Peera, "How the Power of Focus Can Lead You to Success," *Addicted2Success,* November 7, 2014; https://addicted2success .com/motivation/how-the-power-of-focus-can-lead-you-to-success/; accessed January 4, 2020.

9. Geoff Masters, "Learning from Mistakes," *TeacherMagazine,* May 16, 2016; https://www.teachermagazine.com.au/columnists/geoff -masters/learning-from-mistakes; accessed January 10, 2020.

10. James Allen, *As a Man Thinketh* (Kindle Edition accessed April 18, 2018).

11. Brian Scudamore, "Why Successful People Spend 10 Hours a Week Just Thinking," *Inc.com,* April 7, 2016; https://www.inc.com/empact/why-successful-people-spend-10-hours-a-week-just-thinking .html; accessed January 10, 2020.

12. Ibid.

13. Mary Bellis, "The History of the Band-Aid," *ThoughtCo.,* updated March 2, 2019; https://www.thoughtco.com/history-of-the-band -aid-1991345; accessed January 4, 2020.

14. Ibid.

15. Mark Morgan Ford, "How to Become a Great Thinker," *earlytorise .com,* May 23, 2002; https://www.earlytorise.com/how-to-become-a -great-thinker/; accessed January 4, 2020.

Chapter 4

1. Japanese proverb, as quoted in *Civilization's Quotations: Life's Ideal* (2002) by Richard Alan Krieger; https://en.wikiquote.org/wiki/Vision; accessed January 4, 2020.

2. William Douglas and Rubens Teixeira, *The 25 Biblical Laws of Success* (Grand Rapids, MI: Baker Books, 2017), 34.

3. Rick Joyner, *Leadership, Management and the Five Essentials for Success* (Charlotte, NC: MorningStar Publications, 1990, 1995), 51.

4. Burt Nanus, *Visionary Leadership* (San Francisco, CA: Jossey-Bass Publishers, 1992), 135.

5. Ron Bliwas, *The C Student's Guide to Success* (New York: Penguin Group Publishers, 2007), 81-82.

6. Blanche Brick, PhD, quoted by Zig Ziglar, *Over the Top* (Nashville, TN: Thomas Nelson Publishers, 1997), 52.

7. Erik Weihenmayer accomplishments cited in "Blind Mountaineer Conquers the Seven Summits" article on ABCNews.go.com dated January 6, 2006; https://abcnews.go.com/GMA/story?id=125792&page=1; accessed January 4, 2020.

8. Burke Hedges, *You, Inc.* (Tampa, FL: INTI Publishing, 1996), 66.

9. Todd Duncan, *The Power to Be Your Best* (Nashville, TN: Word Publishing, 1999), 140.

10. Earl Nightingale, *The Cure for Procrastination,* http://wordpress.nightingale.com/articles/the-cure-for-procrastination/; accessed January 4, 2020.

11. James Allen, *As a Man Thinketh* (Kindle Edition accessed April 18, 2018).

12. Leith Anderson, *Dying for Change* (Minneapolis, MN: Bethany House Publishers, 1998), 9.

13. Tony Mayo, "The Importance of Vision," *Harvard Business Review,* October 29, 2007; https://hbr.org/2007/10/the-importance-of-vision; accessed January 4, 2020.

Chapter 5

1. Theodore Roosevelt, from speech to the Brotherhood of Locomotive Firemen in Chattanooga, Tennessee; https://en.wikiquote.org/wiki/Theodore_Roosevelt; accessed January 4, 2020.

2. Jay E. House quoted in *The Forbes Book of Business Quotations,* edited by Ted Goodman (New York: Black Dog & Leventhal Publishers, 1997), 804.

3. Ben Carson, *Gifted Hands: The Ben Carson Story* (Grand Rapids, MI: Zondervan, 1996), 232. https://en.wikiquote.org/wiki/Success; accessed January 4, 2020.

4. David Bly quoted in *Peace of Mind: Daily Meditations for Easing Stress* (1995) by Amy Dean; https://en.wikiquote.org/wiki/Work; accessed September 14, 2018.

5. Andrei U, "The Importance of Hard Work in Success," *SelfGrowth.com,* September 4, 2009; https://www.selfgrowth.com/articles/user/188289; accessed September 14, 2018.

6. Burke Hedges, *You, Inc.* (Tampa, FL: INTI Publishing, 1996), 92.

7. Samuel Johnson, as quoted in *Dictionary of burning words of brilliant writers* by Gilbert, Josiah Hotchkiss, 1834- [from old catalog]; https://archive.org/details/dictionaryburni00gilbgoog/page/n310; accessed September 15, 2018.

8. Robert Taibbi, "How to Break Bad Habits," *Psychology Today,* December 15, 2017; https://www.psychologytoday.com/us/blog/fixing-families/201712/how-break-bad-habits; accessed January 4, 2020.

9. James Clear, "How Long Does It Actually Take to Form a New Habit? (Backed by Science)" quoted from the study conducted and published in the *European Journal of Social Psychology.* Complete study can be accessed @https://onlinelibrary.wiley.com/; https://jamesclear.com/new-habit; accessed January 4, 2020.

10. Earl Riney quoted in *The Forbes Book of Business Quotations,* edited by Ted Goodman, (New York: Black Dog & Leventhal Publishers, 1997), 240.

11. Groucho Marx quoted in November 3, 1954, *Greensboro Record, Inside TV* by Eve Starr, Quote Page B3, Column 4, Greensboro, NC (Genealogy Bank); https://quoteinvestigator.com/2014/05/17/angry-speech/#return-note-8894-1; accessed September 19, 2018.

12. "Quotes of the Day: Comedian Buddy Hackett On Forgiveness," *Investor's Business Daily;* https://www.investors.com/news/management/wisdom-to-live-by/famous-quotes-by-buddy-hackett-and-patti-labelle/; accessed January 4, 2020.

13. Zameena Mejia and Marguerite Ward, "Warren Buffett says this one investment 'supersedes all others'"; https://www.cnbc.com/2017/10/04/warren-buffett-says-this-one-investment-supersedes-all-others.html; accessed January 4, 2020.

14. Charles "T" Jones, *Life is Tremendous,* (Harrisburg, PA.,Executive Books, 1968) p. 73

15. Julie Blim and Lisa Ryan, "Joel Osteen: The Power of Positivity (part 2)," *The Christian Broadcasting Network;* https://www1.cbn.com/700club/joel-osteen-power-positivity-part-2; accessed January 4, 2020.

Chapter 6

1. Esther Ewing, "What golf has taught me about leadership," *The Globe and Mail,* August 3, 2015; https://www.theglobeandmail.com/report-on-business/careers/leadership-lab/what-golf-has-taught-me-about-leadership/article25750788/; accessed January 6, 2020.

2. Daniel Newman, Principal Analyst of Futurum Research and the CEO of Broadsuite Media Group, "7 Critical Leadership Lessons that can be Learned on the Golf Course," *Future of Work,* August 29, 2011; https://fowmedia.com/7-critical-leadership-lessons-learned -golf/; accessed January 6, 2020.

3. Jeffrey Carter, "Fundamentals Are Important," *Points and Figures,* March 26, 2016; http://pointsandfigures.com/2016/03/26/fundamentals-are-important; accessed January 6, 2020.

4. Sean Foley, "Take Your Game from the Range to the Course," *GolfDigest,* June 8, 2017; https://www.golfdigest.com/story/take -your-game-from-the-range-to-the-course; accessed January 6, 2020.

5. Peter Jacobsen quoted in *Forbes* article "Golf: The Game of Life" by Brent Beshore, August 20, 2012; https://www.forbes.com/sites/brentbeshore/2012/08/20/golf-the-game-of-life/#2f2445f84bcf; accessed January 6, 2020.

6. Ibid.

7. Bob Rotella quoted in *GolfDigest* article, "Do tour pros really need swing coaches, anyway?" by Jaime Diaz, February 27, 2017; https://www.golfdigest.com/story/do-tour-pros-really-need-swing-coaches -anyway; accessed January 6, 2020.

8. David F. Larcker, et.al., "2013 Executive Coaching Survey," The Miles Group and Stanford University, August 2013 (accessed January 6, 2020). Author's Note: To download full survey: https://www.gsb.stanford.edu/faculty-research/publications/2013-executive-coaching-survey.

9. Lolly Daskal, "Why Your Emerging Leaders Need Coaching"; https://www.lollydaskal.com/leadership/emerging-leaders-need -coaching/; accessed January 7, 2020.

10. Kathryn Belanger, "Why the Rules Matter" *USGA.org,* January 28, 2016; https://www.usga.org/articles/2016/01/the-rules-of-golf--why -they-matter.html; accessed January 7, 2020.

11. Warren Bennis, *Managing People Is Like Herding Cats* (Provo, UT: Executive Excellence Pub., 1997), 98.

12. Terry Orlick, PhD, *In Pursuit of Excellence* (Champaign, IL: Human Kinetics Pub., 4th Edition, 2008), 282.

13. Ibid., 171.

14. Malcolm Gladwell, *Outliers: The Story of Success* (New York: Little, Brown, and Co., 2008), 41.

Chapter 7

1. Skip Prichard, "9 Qualities of the Servant Leader," January 24, 2013; https://www.skipprichard.com/9-qualities-of-the-servant-leader/; accessed January 7, 2020.

2. Cheryl Cole, a judge on the UK version of "The X Factor, The Xtra Factor," November 23, 2009; https://www.youtube.com/watch?v=daMn4zJxPXY; accessed November 1, 2018.

3. Akintola Benson-Oke, "Unlocking the 'X Factor' in leadership," *Vanguard,* March 6, 2017; https://www.vanguardngr.com/2017/03/unlocking-x-factor-leadership/; accessed January 6, 2020.

4. Suzanne Bates and David Casullo, "Executive Presence: The Elusive 'X Factor' in Leadership," *Chief Executive,* May 7, 2014; https://chiefexecutive.net/executive-presence-the-elusive-x-factor-in-leadership/; accessed January 5, 2020.

5. Thomas Jefferson; https://en.wikiquote.org/wiki/Integrity; accessed November 2, 2018.

6. Mick Ukleja, "6 Attributes of Healthy Humility," *SUCCESS,* November 25, 2016; https://www.success.com/6-attributes-of-healthy-humility/; accessed January 5, 2020.

7. Mac Davis, "It's Hard to be Humble," Casablanca label, 1980; BMG Rights Management.

8. Rob McKinnon, "The X-Factor of Great Leadership: Why Humility Comes First"; http://mckinnoncompany.com/x-factor-great-leadership; accessed January 5, 2020.

9. Michael Johnson, Terry Mitchell, Bradley Owens, "Humility is a key to high performance and effective leadership," *University of Washington Foster School of Business,* September 19, 2012; https://foster.uw.edu/research-brief/humility-is-a-key-to-high-performance-and-effective-leadership/; accessed January 6, 2020.

10. Craig Impelman, "The Qualities of a Humble Leader," *SUCCESS,* December 27, 2017; quoted from *How to Be Like Coach Wooden: Life Lessons from Basketball's Greatest Leader* by Pat Williams (Deerfield Beach, FL: Health Communications, 2006). Impelman's article: https://www.success.com/the-qualities-of-a-humble-leader; accessed January 7, 2020.

11. Thuy Sindell, PhD and Milo Sindell, MS, "The Golden Rule of Leadership: Leading others is a privilege, not a right," *Psychology Today,* June 6, 2013; https://www.psychologytoday.com/us/blog/the -end -work-you-know-it/201306/the-golden-rule-leadership; accessed January 6, 2020.

12. George S. Patton quoted in *I Remember General Patton's Principles* (1984) by Porter B. Williamson; https://en.wikiquote.org/wiki/ George_S._Patton; accessed November 4, 2018.

13. Robert K. Greenleaf, "What is Servant Leadership?" *Center for Servant Leadership;* https://www.greenleaf.org/what-is-servant -leadership/; accessed January 6, 2020.

14. Michael Hyatt, "How Real Leaders Demonstrate Accountability"; https://michaelhyatt.com/leadership-and-accountability; accessed January 6, 2020.

15. Dr. Everett Piper, President, Oklahoma Wesleyan University, *This is Not a Day Care. It's a University!* https://www.okwu.edu/ blog/2015/11/; accessed November 13, 2018. (Author's Note: This letter has been published and reprinted on many websites yet is not now available on the university's website. Dr. Piper retired as OWU president June 1, 2019. His book *Not a Day Care: The Devastating Consequences of Abandoning Truth* was published 2017 (Washington, DC: Salem Books, 2017). Hardcover and Kindle edition available on Amazon.com.

16. Charles "T" Jones, *Life is Tremendous*, (Harrisburg, PA.,Executive Books, 1968) p. 26.

17. Laci Lowe, "Leadership Development Today," *Brandon Hall Group,* December 10, 2014; http://www.brandonhall.com/blogs/the-buck -stops-here-a-culture-of-accountability-drives-effective-leadership/; accessed January 6, 2020.

Chapter 8

1. Robert R. Gilruth, "I Believe We Should Go to the Moon" in the book *Apollo Expeditions to the Moon: The NASA History;* https://www.hq.nasa.gov/office/pao/History/SP-350/ch-2-1.html; accessed January 6, 2020.

2. George Bradt, "Intentional Leaders Are Not Victims of Circumstance," *Forbes,* April 23, 2012; https://www.forbes.com/sites/georgebradt/2012/04/23/intentional-leaders-are-not-victims-of-circumstance; accessed January 6, 2020.

3. Dr. Randy Carlson, *The Power of One Thing* (Carol Stream, IL: Tyndale House Pub., 2009), 32.

4. Thomas A. Edison quotes, http://www.quoteauthors.com/thomas-a-edison-quote/; accessed November 23, 2018.

5. Dr. Randy Carlson, *The Power of One Thing,* 15.

6. Gary Keller, *The ONE Thing* (Austin, TX: Bard Press, 2012), 44.

7. William Yardley, "Clifford Nass, Who Warned of a Data Deluge, Dies at 55," *The New York Times, November* 6, 2013; https://www.nytimes.com/2013/11/07/business/clifford-nass-researcher-on-multitasking-dies-at-55.html; accessed January 7, 2020.

8. Steve Uzzell quoted by Gary Keller, *The ONE Thing,* 44.

9. Stephen R. Covey, A. Roger Merrill, Rebecca R. Merrill, *First Things First* (New York: Simon & Schuster, 1994), 18.

10. Tim Kimmel, *Little House on the Freeway* (Colorado Springs, CO: Multnomah Books, 2008), 143.

11. Cristy Lane; https://genius.com/Cristy-lane-one-day-at-a-time-lyrics; accessed December 2, 2018).

12. John Mason, *You Can Be Your Best,* https://books.google.com/books; accessed December 10, 2018.

13. Kirk Nugent, *Pursue Your Passion,* Public Speech; http://www.youtube.com/watch?v=K4wDVrfLIq0 5:10/6:17 (2007); https://en.wikiquote.org/wiki/Passion; accessed December 3, 2018.

14. Hyman G. Rickover quoted in *The Rickover Effect* (1992) by Theodore Rockwell. https://en.wikiquote.org/wiki/Responsibility; accessed December 3, 2018.

15. Zig Ziglar, *Over the Top* (Nashville, TN: Thomas Nelson, 1997), 47.

16. Dr. Randy Carlson, *The Power of One Thing,* 193.

17. ZURB blog, Interview with Nike CEO, Mark Parker, *Crappy Stuff for Good Stuff,* https://zurb.com/blog/steve-jobs-innovation-is-saying-no-to-1-0; accessed January 10, 2020.

Chapter 9

1. As reported in Josiah Hotchkiss Gilbert's *Dictionary of Burning Words of Brilliant Writers* (New York: W. B. Ketcham Publishers, 1895), 450.

2. Aesop's greatest fables, *The Tortoise and the Hare,* http://www.storyarts.org/library/aesops/stories/tortoise.html; accessed February 1, 2019.

3. Ben Chodos, "10 Greatest Upsets in Summer Olympic History," *BleacherReport.com;* https://bleacherreport.com/articles/1171485-the-10-greatest-upsets-in-summer-olympic-history; accessed January 7, 2020.

4. Steven K. Scott, *The Richest Man Who Ever Lived* (New York: Doubleday, 2006), 13.

5. "Diligence: The Key Ingredient to Success," *kavikishor.com;* http://www.kavikishor.com/2016/diligence-the-key-ingredient-to-success.html; accessed January 7, 2020.

6. Diligent vs Persistent—What's the difference?; https://wikidiff.com/diligent/persistent; accessed February 4, 2019.

7. "Winston Churchill's speech before the House of Commons following the disaster at Dunkirk, June 4, 1940," *AHC;* storyonthenet.com/authentichistory/1939-1945/1-war/1-39-41/19400604_Churchill_Address_to_HOC_on_Dunkirk.html; accessed January 7, 2020.

8. *The Forbes Book of Business Quotations*, edited by Ted Goodman (New York: Black Dog & Leventhal Publishing, 1997), 645.

9. http://characterfirsteducation.com/c/curriculum-detail/2050435; accessed February 4, 2019.

10. *The Forbes Book of Business Quotations*, 646.

11. "The World's Smallest Preacher (Prov. 6:6-11)," *First Baptist Church,* 2007; http://www.fbcstamps.com/the_worlds_smallest_preacher_prov6611; accessed January 7, 2020.

12. Dan Charney, "Employers Want Self-Starters"; https://www.directrecruiters.com/dri-candidate-advice/employers-want-you-to-be-a-self-starter/; accessed January 7, 2020.

Chapter 10

1. https://en.wikiquote.org/wiki/Alan_K._Simpson; accessed April 18, 2019.

2. Amy Rees Anderson, "Success Will Come and Go, But Integrity Is Forever"; http://www.amyreesanderson.com/blog/success-will-come -and-go-but-integrity-is-forever/#.XhSy4KzsZpw; accessed January 7, 2020.

3. Dr. Dave Martin, *The 12 Traits of the Greats* (Tulsa, OK: Harrison House Publishers, 2011), 194.

4. Msgr. Charles Pope, "What Does Jesus Mean by Hypocrisy? It's Deeper than You Think," *Community in Mission* blog; February 23, 2012; http://blog.adw.org/2012/02/what-does-jesus-mean-by -hypocrisy; accessed January 7, 2020.

5. Dr. Dave Martin, *The 12 Traits of the Greats*, 200.

6. https://www.inc.com/marcel-schwantes/first-90-days-warren -buffetts-advice-for-hiring-based-on-3-traits.html; accessed April 20, 2019.

7. https://www.inc.com/lolly-daskal/the-100-best-leadership-quotes-of -all-time; accessed April 23, 2019.

8. Nick Unsworth, "The Importance of Integrity: Now More Than Ever," *Entrepreneur,* January 2, 2018; https://www.entrepreneur.com/ article/305640; accessed January 7, 2020.

9. Bob Warters, "Calling a Penalty on Yourself," *GolfMagic,* November 27, 2008; https://www.golfmagic.com/news/golf-news/calling-a -penalty-on-yourself/5955; accessed January 7, 2020.

10. Steven Mintz, "Do the Ends Justify the Means?" *Ethics Sage*, April 3, 2018; https://www.ethicssage.com/2018/04/do-the-ends-justify-the -means.html; accessed January 7, 2020.

11. https://www.biblestudytools.com/topical-verses/bible-verses-about -honesty-and-integrity/; accessed January 7, 2020.

12. https://www.yourdictionary.com/about/websters-new-world-college -dictionary.html; accessed April 24, 2019.

13. George S. Patton quoted at https://en.wikiquote.org/wiki/Loyalty; accessed January 7, 2020.

14. Todd Duncan, *The Power to be Your Best* (Nashville, TN: Word Publishing, 1999), 232.

15. Bill Purvis, "Three Ways to Maintain Your Integrity & Strengthen Your Character"; https://www1.cbn.com/3-ways-to-maintain -integrity-and-character; accessed January 7, 2020.

Chapter 11

1. Asa Don Brown, PhD, "Toxic Relationships," *Psychology Today;* https://www.psychologytoday.com/us/blog/towards-recovery; accessed June 13, 2019.
2. Ibid.
3. Carolyn Steber, *11 Subtle Differences Between A Toxic Relationship Vs. One That Just Needs Work*, https://www.bustle.com/; accessed June 13, 2019.
4. Len Sweet quote from an article at https://housetohouse.com/; accessed June 13, 2019.
5. Debbie McDaniel, "How to Protect Yourself from These 10 Toxic People," *Crosswalk.com,* September 3, 2019; https://www.crosswalk .com/faith/women/how-to-protect-yourself-from-these-10-toxic -people.html; accessed January 8, 2020.
6. http://picdeer.com/changinglifequotes1; accessed June 14, 2019.

Chapter 12

1. Jim Rohn, *The Treasury of Quotes* (Irving, TX: Jim Rohn International, 1994), 32.
2. https://www.quotes.net/quote/4028; accessed August 27, 2019.
3. https://en.wikiquote.org/wiki/Optimism; accessed August 27, 2019.

Chapter 13

1. Lydia Sweatt, "11 Quotes About Leaving a Legacy," *SUCCESS,* December 8, 2016; https://www.success.com/11-quotes-about -leaving-a-legacy; accessed January 9, 2020.
2. Kimberly Wade-Benzoni, "How to Think About Building Your Legacy," *Harvard Business Review,* December 15, 2016; https://hbr .org/2016/12/how-to-think-about-building-your-legacy; accessed January 9, 2020.
3. Lydia Sweatt, "11 Quotes About Leaving a Legacy," *SUCCESS,* December 8, 2016; https://www.success.com/11-quotes-about -leaving-a-legacy/; accessed January 9, 2020.

4. "Legacy," https://www.merriam-webster.com/dictionary/legacy/; accessed January 11, 2020.

5. Lydia Sweatt; https://www.success.com/11-quotes-about-leaving-a-legacy/; accessed January 9, 2020).

6. *Business Dictionary;* http://www.businessdictionary.com/definition/strategy.html; accessed January 9, 2020.

7. *Veritas Strategies;* https://www.veritasstrategies.com/resource-center/lifestyle/building-your-legacy; accessed January 9, 2020.

8. J. Oswald Sanders, *Spiritual Leadership* (Chicago, IL: Moody Publishers, 2007), 50-51.

9. Laurie Beth Jones, *Jesus CEO* (New York: Hyperion, 1995), 150-151.

10. https://www.deseretnews.com/article/700252819/Olympics-Americans-drop-baton-chance-at-medal; accessed July 6, 2019.

11. James G. Poitras, "Passing the Baton from Generation to Generation," August 5, 2012, *Leadership Development International;* Tony Wang quoted from "Passing the Baton"; https://developandlead.com/2012/08/05/passing-the-baton-from-generation-to-generation/; accessed January 9, 2020.

12. Susan V. Bosak, "What is Legacy?"; https://www.legacyproject.org/guides/whatislegacy.html; accessed January 9, 2020.

13. Bill High, "7 Great Quotes on Leaving a Legacy," https://billhigh.com/legacy/7-great-quotes-on-leaving-a-legacy; accessed January 9, 2020.

14. "The Power of Character," *CharacterTraining.com;* https://www.character-training.com/blog; accessed January 9, 2020.

Epilogue

1. Warren Bennis, *Managing People Is Like Herding Cats* (Provo, UT: Executive Excellence Publishing, 1997), 104.

2. Ibid., 103.

3. J. Oswald Sanders, *Spiritual Leadership* (Chicago, IL: Moody Publishers, 2007), 37.

4. R.E. Thompson, in *World Vision,* December 1966, 4.

5. Sanders, *Spiritual Leadership*, 37-41.

About the Author

Paul and Billie Kaye Tsika have been involved in ministry for more than forty-five years. He has authored several books including: *What You Seed Is What You Get, Sequoia-Size Success, Releasing Your Full Potential,* and *The Overcomer's Edge.* Together they have authored books including: *Growing in Favor; Get Married, Stay Married;* and *Parenting with Purpose.* Paul has been the pastor of a large international marketing business since 2001. Along with their staff, they minister to tens of thousands of people each year and witness many coming to Christ for salvation. They reside at Restoration Ranch in Texas.

OTHER DESTINY IMAGE BOOKS BY PAUL TSIKA

The Overcomer's Edge: Strategies for Victorious Living in 13 Key Areas of Life

Growing in Grace: Daily Devotions for Hungry Hearts

OTHER DESTINY IMAGE BOOKS BY PAUL TSIKA AND BILLIE KAYE TSIKA

Parenting with Purpose: Winning the Heart of Your Child

Get Married, Stay Married

OTHER DESTINY IMAGE BOOKS BY BILLIE KAYE TSIKA

Priceless: A Woman of Strength